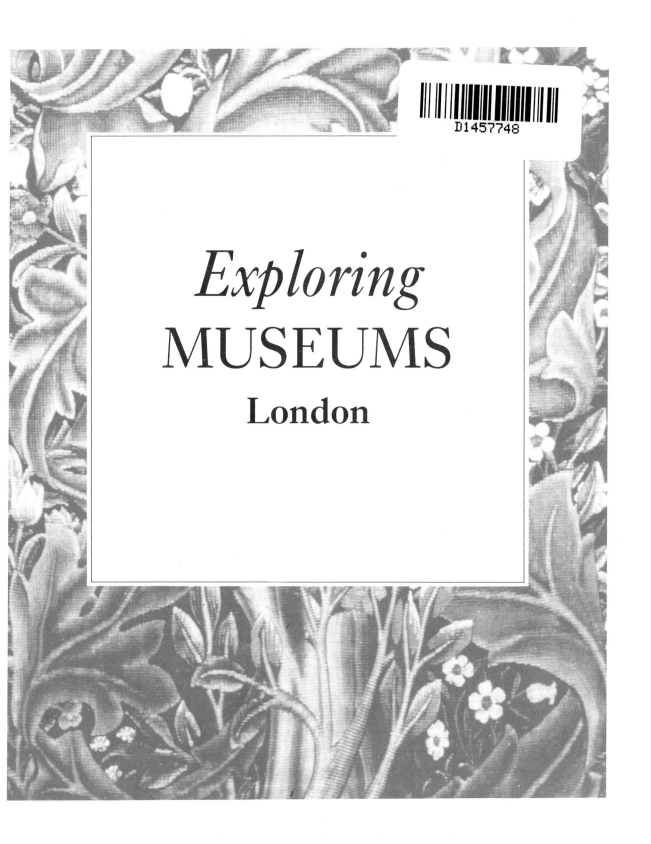

Exploring
MUSEUMS
London

MUSEUMS & GALLERIES COMMISSION

A MUSEUMS ASSOCIATION GUIDE

Exploring MUSEUMS

London

Simon Olding

LONDON: HER MAJESTY'S STATIONERY OFFICE

© Crown Copyright 1989

First published 1989

ISBN 0 11 290465 3

British Library Cataloguing in
Publication Data
A CIP catalogue record for this book is
available from the British Library

HMSO publications are available from:

HMSO Publications Centre
(Mail and telephone orders only)
PO Box 276, London, SW8 5DT
Telephone orders 01–873 9090
General enquiries 01–873 0011
(queuing system in operation for both numbers)

HMSO Bookshops
49 High Holborn, London, WC1V 6HB 01–873 0011 (Counter service only)
258 Broad Street, Birmingham, B1 2HE 021–643 3740
Southey House, 33 Wine Street, Bristol, BS1 2BQ (0272) 264306
9–21 Princess Street, Manchester, M60 8AS 061–834 7201
80 Chichester Street, Belfast, BT1 4JY (0232) 238451
71 Lothian Road, Edinburgh, EH3 9AZ 031–228 4181

HMSO's Accredited Agents
(see Yellow Pages)

and through good booksellers

CONTENTS

OTHER VOLUMES IN THE SERIES

South West England
Arnold Wilson (former Director of
Bristol City Art Gallery)
ISBN 0 11 290469 6

**North West England
and the Isle of Man**
David Phillips (Lecturer, Art
Gallery and Museum Studies,
University of Manchester)
ISBN 0 11 290473 4

North East England
David Fleming (Principal Keeper
of Museums, Hull City Museums
and Art Galleries)
ISBN 0 11 290470 X

The Home Counties
Geoff Marsh, Nell Hoare and
Karen Hull (Museums
Development Officers, AMSSEE)
ISBN 0 11 290471 8

The Midlands
Tim Schadla-Hall (Deputy
Director, Leicestershire
Museums, Art Galleries and
Records Service)
ISBN 0 11 290466 1

East Anglia
Alf Hatton (Lecturer in Museum
Studies at the University of
London)
ISBN 0 11 290472 6

**Southern England
and the Channel Islands**
Kenneth James Barton (former
Director of Hampshire County
Museums Service)
ISBN 0 11 290468 8

Scotland
Colin Thompson (former Director
of National Galleries of Scotland
and former Chairman of the
Scottish Museums Council)
ISBN 0 11 290474 2

Ireland
Seán Popplewell (Executive
Director, Irish Museums Trust)
ISBN 0 11 290475 0

Wales
Geraint Jenkins (Curator, Welsh
Folk Museum)
ISBN 0 11 290467 X

BUCKINGHAM PALACE

As Patron of Museums Year 1989, I hope that through this series
of Regional Guides "Exploring Museums", you will derive great enjoyment
from the fascinating world of museums and galleries; there are some
two thousand of them offering an immense variety and range of experiences
so there is something for everyone. It is so exciting to feel the
sense of exploring new areas in the world of museums and galleries.
Make the most of what is on offer in 1989.

Sarah.

January 1989

EDITOR'S NOTE

This volume is one of a series of eleven regional guides to museums in the British Isles. The term 'museum' is often applied to a wide variety of collections and buildings: most of the places selected for description in the *Exploring Museums* guides, however, comply as far as possible with the Museums Association's definition of a museum as 'an institution that collects, documents, preserves, exhibits and interprets material evidence and associated information for the public benefit'.

Given the sheer quantity of museums in the British Isles, the guides describe only a selection, concentrating on those places that authors considered most worthy of a visit, either because of the quality of their collections and displays, or because of the interesting or unusual nature of what they have on view. Museums in each area not described in full are listed at the back of the guides, with brief details of their collections; please note that some of these are only open by appointment. The lists include new museums that are scheduled to open in the near future.

The principal aim of this series is to describe, through words and pictures, the types of things that visitors can expect to see and do at various museums. Authors have tried to put themselves in the shoes of a general museum visitor, and present a personal rather than an official view in their descriptions. It should be noted that specific items they describe may not be on show when you visit: most museums now change their displays fairly often, and if you want to see something in particular you should check beforehand with the museum concerned. Most of the illustrations have been selected by the authors, and highlight lesser-known objects and museum activities, as well as exhibits for which particular museums are renowned. Basic information about access and facilities has been kept to a minimum, as opening times or bus routes, for example, are frequently subject to change; please check with museums before visiting for precise details of opening times, holiday closures, admission prices, and how to get there, and for information on special events and activities.

Krystyna Matyjaszkiewicz
Series Editor

*The views expressed in this guide are those of
the author and not necessarily those of the Museums Association.*

FOREWORD

President of the Museums Association
Patrick Boylan
and the Chairman of the Museums & Galleries Commission
Brian Morris

This series is being published in Museums Year 1989, which marks the centenary of the Museums Association. When the Association's first conference was held in York in 1889, there were already several hundred museums in Britain. Now there are some 2,300, and new ones are opening every month. They vary enormously in size and scope, from the large all-purpose museum to the small collection in a converted house. Many of the smaller museums are less well known than they should be, and it is these particularly that the books in this series seek to highlight.

Museums Year 1989, sponsored by The Times newspaper, represents the most significant promotion of the country's museums and galleries ever staged. Through their sponsorship Museums Year will bring fresh vitality to a particularly important part of our British heritage.

Never before have museums in general been as popular as they are today. In 1989 alone they are expected to receive between them something like 100 million visits (which is more than any sport or other leisure activity). They are especially attractive to young people, to the curious of all ages and to the lovers of beautiful, unusual and exciting things. There are indeed museums for every taste and interest, for every day and in every area. We are sure that these books will help many more people to discover the museums of Britain, to learn from them and to enjoy them.

INTRODUCTION

London is the museum capital of the world. There are perhaps three hundred museums and new museum projects scattered all over the capital, and a constant popular movement to increase that number. Every month, it seems, a new idea for a museum surfaces: a museum for Florence Nightingale, a collection of vehicles shown in a police garage, a restored beam engine, or a local history museum for a London Borough.

London has no plan for this spontaneous and unrelenting growth: it simply acts as a huge cultural magnet drawing in visitors, projects and ideas. Certainly museums in London are increasing in popularity (well over twenty million visits are made to museums in the capital in a year) and big new projects receive significant press coverage.

The range of museums in the capital is extraordinary. The great national collections hardly need an introduction. These museums – the **National Gallery**, **Natural History Museum**, **Victoria and Albert Museum**, **Science Museum**, and **British Museum** – host major exhibitions as a matter of course (and a matter of cultural duty), and they retain a magisterial character enforced by huge buildings and astonishing collections.

But there is another museum community in London – less well known, perhaps, but still full of surprises and delights. This community is made up of specialist collections, site-museums, local history displays, and historic houses. The purpose of this guide, and the selection of museums within, is to draw attention to this world. There are small museums in the centre of London, as well as throughout the outer boroughs, that are often much less forbidding places in themselves, and will certainly be quieter, and offer an unrivalled range of subjects, themes, and collections.

These smaller museums often stand as a testament to the pride of a local authority, an individual, or a local history society – all keen to preserve their past, and to symbolise their care for ways of life that are fast disappearing. It is difficult, otherwise, to account for the prolific amount of small museums devoted to restoring London's industrial archaeology (pumping stations and beam engines are increasingly used as sites for museums). Common, too, is the 'historic house' approach, and collections devoted to **Freud**, Marx, and Benjamin Franklin have all recently been developed. Museums concerning subjects as diverse as the fan, the taxi, or gas all figure in this world. So do local history museums for the London Boroughs, which have recently been opening at a regular rate. These form a particularly interesting part of the museum community, since curators of these new borough museums (such as **Hackney** or **Wandsworth**) are telling much more approachable and relevant stories about local history.

This selection of museums aims to give an accurate idea of the nature and content of museum collections across London. The range of subjects that has been covered by the sixty main entries is therefore purposefully wide, including social history, art, and military or religious life. The geographical spread has also been a factor in the selection, and whilst inevitably there is a concentration of museums, large and very small, in the centre of London, there are other 'museum trails' in the outer boroughs. The great historic house museums of west London (from *Hogarth's House* to **Orleans House** and *Ham House*) make one group with an architectural theme. A more varied museum excursion could be made along the London Underground Northern Line, taking in the **RAF Museum** at Hendon, and stopping off along the route at **Church Farm House** and **Keats House**.

It is certainly worth emphasising the advances that are being made in many small museums in London to improve the standard of displays for the public, and this selection includes the best of recently-opened or newly redisplayed museums. Those museums that have developed a more open approach to their visitors, whether by a welcoming museum attendant or a particularly good range of educational activities, have also been included.

Simon Olding

ACKNOWLEDGEMENTS

Author's acknowledgements

I owe particular debts of gratitude to Julie Ackland, Lesley Hackett, Isabel Hughes and Crispin Paine for their advice, support, and practical help. I should also like to thank all of the curators, guides and attendants who always make me a welcome visitor to their museums.

Photographic acknowledgements

The Museums Association is grateful to all the museums, archives and photographers who generously provided material for illustration herein. Photographs were supplied by, and are reproduced courtesy of, the respective museums and their governing bodies or Trustees, except for those noted below.

p. 4, Map of Elizabethan Exeter © copyright The British Library Board; pp. 6–7, Charles Darwin Memorial Museum photographs © copyright Down House and the Royal College of Surgeons of England; p. 8, Church Farm House Museum photographs by David Bicknell; p. 17, photograph of Sigmund Freud reproduced by permission of AW Freud et al, by arrangement with Sigmund Freud Copyrights; p. 18, John Piper, *The Geffrye Museum in Autumn*, limited edition print reproduced courtesy of the Friends of the Geffrye Museum; p. 21, painting by Dan Jones is *Demonstrators outside the Grunwick photographic processing works in Chapter Road, Willesden, during the long dispute over union recognition in 1977*, 1978; p. 22, photograph of soldiers marching © copyright Imperial War Museum; p. 24, detail of photograph by Ed Barber of a machinist at the Kikku Jeans Factory, Southall, 1987, part of the Gunnersbury Park Museum project *A Stitch in Time*, funded by GLA; p. 25, photograph of builders courtesy of Hackney Archives Department; pp. 38–39, Keats House photographs by Keith Wynn, © copyright Photocraft (Hampstead) Ltd; p. 40, Lady's Court Dress, 1912 [loaned by Royal Albert Memorial Museum, Exeter], and uniform of King's Bodyguard for Scotland (Royal Company of Archers), 1912; p. 40, Wedding dress of Lady Diana Spencer reproduced courtesy of Her Royal Highness The Princess of Wales; p. 45, Women's day trip reproduced courtesy of Southwark Local Studies Library; p. 46, *Light at the Livesey* photograph, Blackfriars Photography Project; p. 61, photograph of Sade © copyright and courtesy of Johnny Rozsa; p. 70, Design for East Front of Pitshanger Museum © copyright and courtesy of the Trustees of Sir John Soane's Museum; p. 74, Arnold Dolmetsch Green Harpsichord reproduced courtesy of The Horniman Museum and Library; p. 81, photograph of 13 Lincoln's Inn Fields by Professor Margaret Harker; p. 82, Barry Flanagan sculpture © copyright and reproduced courtesy of the artist; p. 83, David Hockney painting © copyright and reproduced courtesy of the artist; p. 83, Claes Oldenburg © copyright and reproduced courtesy of the artist; p. 84, Edward Burra painting © copyright the artist; p. 86, Robert Canning in the Queensland Ballet's *Savage Earth*, 1987, detail of photograph by Derrick George, exhibited at the Theatre Museum in 1988; pp. 93–94 and colour plate 3, Westminster Abbey Museum photographs © copyright the Dean and Chapter of Westminster.

Key to Symbols Used

For general location:

⊖ Nearest London Underground station

⇌ Nearest British Rail station

(please check with museums for precise details of how to get there)

◪ Free admission

◪ Admission charge

▼ Voluntary donation requested

◪ Restaurant/cafeteria on premises

◪ Car Park on premises

◪ Good access and facilities for disabled

♿ Difficult/limited access and facilities for disabled and infirm

> **W** Unstepped access via main or side door, wheelchair spaces, and adapted toilet
>
> **T** Adapted toilet
>
> **X** Flat or one-step access
>
> **A** Access with 2–5 steps, or split level exhibition space
>
> **S** Many unavoidable steps and/or other obstacles for wheelchair users and the infirm
>
> **G** Provision made for guide dogs
>
> (based on disabled access code devised by ARTSLINE (01 388 2227), the free telephone information service on the arts in Greater London for people with disabilities)

◪ Group visits

♟ School group visits

◎ Workshops/holiday events/guided tours/talks – 'phone for details

Museums shown in **bold** type in the text are described in full elsewhere in the volume; those shown in *italic* type are briefly described in the list of museums and collections at the back.

Bethnal Green Museum of Childhood

Cambridge Heath Road, London
E2 9PA   01-980 3204/4315
⊖ Bethnal Green ⇌ Cambridge
Heath
Closed Fridays. 🇫 🅿
♿ W G: access to first floor by
steps; wheelchair users can
make arrangements in advance.
🚻 🍴 pre-book only if a talk
required; details and booking form
in Teachers' Pack. ☺

A Butcher's shop, 19th century

Standing in the Toy Gallery of this fine and cheerful museum, listening to the echoes of delighted cries from crowds of children, is a heartening experience for every museum worker who believes in making the public enjoy themselves while learning.

The Bethnal Green Museum of Childhood (run as a branch of the Victoria and Albert Museum) houses the national collection of historic toys, dolls, puppets, and children's dress, in a fine open-plan building. The latter is

Interior view (Bethnal Green Museum)

itself historically important, as it was the first building to house the South Kensington Museum (now the Victoria and Albert Museum), and was dismantled, removed and rebuilt on its current site in the East End of London. It is now one of the last surviving examples of a type of pre-fabricated iron and glass construction used by Joseph Paxton in the Great Exhibition building of 1851, which was also dismantled and rebuilt on another site that became known as Crystal Palace.

The layout of the museum is informal, though not haphazard, and types of objects are grouped together (for example toy soldiers, puppets and toy theatre, dolls' houses, and so on) in a way that encourages a relaxed visit. Being able to see the whole span of the museum at one glance enhances the atmosphere of light and airy space. The building is large enough to encourage a good half-day visit with children, yet not so big that it becomes frustrating. Every visitor will leave with special memories: mine was watching Albert the Lion work. This cheerfully morbid automaton by Michael Howard (1983) is activated by a coin, which opens up the lion's body to show a captured victim's legs going up and down as he screams in unison with the

lion's tail wagging. A small group of children watched this macabre sight with silent fascination.

The museum displays are full of equally attractive (and sometimes bizarre) objects. In the toy galleries there are superb and meticulously-made 19th century Noah's Arks, great regiments of cast-lead soldiers, impressive layouts of clockwork railways, and other historic automata. There is an international collection of puppets and toy theatre, with an artful display of shadow puppets, and a large collection of fully-constructed toy theatres.

One of the greatest treasures of the museum is contained in the impressive collection of dolls' houses – the beautifully-made Nuremberg house of 1673. Very few examples of these, the earliest dolls' houses, have survived, and this is the only one that can be seen by the public outside Germany. Other British dolls' houses on display range from grand houses furnished by royalty, to ones such as 'Mrs Bryant's Pleasure', an outstandingly accurate interior of an 1860s house (made for adults rather than children), and two endearing 1930s holiday villas.

To accompany the houses there is a large collection of dolls arranged in chronological order. The displays con-

A selection from the Bethnal Green Museum's collection of modern craft toys

The British Museum

*Great Russell Street, London
WC1B 3DG   01-636 1555
Recorded information 01-580 1788*
⊖ Tottenham Court Road, Russell Square, Holborn
Closed Sunday mornings; essential work may necessitate closing certain areas without notice. ⏣ ▣
⅙ W G: most parts of museum accessible by wheelchair; limited disabled car parking and wheel-chairs available by prior arrange-ment; access guide and further information from Education Service (ext. 8511).
⍟ & ⍟ contact Education Service (ext. 8511) to book visits and obtain advice and material. ◎

centrate as much on the appearance of undressed dolls, to show how they were made, as on the elaborately-clothed examples of fashion dolls. Some were modelled on real people and look very accurate, like the portrait doll of Lord Roberts (army Com-mander-in Chief in India and during the Boer War). Others bear only a passing resemblance to the people they represent, for example the 'Shirley Temple Doll' modelled on the film star by the Ideal Novelty and Toy Company in the 1930s.

The museum has recently com-pleted the rearrangement of its first three galleries; the shop and temporary exhibition area on the ground floor have particularly snappy and bright

Children playing with a dolls' house during special activities

modern exhibitions, and display cases echoing the original ironwork. The top floor of the museum is currently in the process of complete reorganization, with a programme called 'The Child-hood Project' that intends to look at the social history of childhood. The dis-plays here will show the material evi-dence of childhood in a historical con-text, rather than exhibiting objects solely for their own sake. Themes such as schooling, diet, dress, play, and parental attitudes will be covered in an ambitious way, and the gallery prom-ises to be an important and pioneering development in the museum world. At present it has temporary displays of costumes, prams, and cradles. The children's costume collection has ex-amples from the 18th century to the present day, including rare early outfits of silk woven nearby in Spitalfields, and the complete wardrobe that young Henrietta Byron wore in 1840.

The Bethnal Green Museum of Childhood tries not to be a place where children (or adults) arrive and look solemnly at objects behind glass cases. Interactive exhibits, though few at pre-sent, will be increased; the Education Department runs an exciting program-me of activities and events, from Satur-day workshops in the Art Room to special holiday events.

If a journalist for British television wants to get an instant reaction repre-senting the voice of common opinion, there are two likely places to go: a London taxi rank, or the forecourt of the British Museum. You may not be hailed by a television crew on your way to the museum, but you will certainly

The Portland Vase, late 1st century BC

Detail of an Assyrian relief, 1st century BC

Bronze warrior on horseback, probably made in Taranto c. 550 BC

Albrecht Durer, An Elk, *1519*

at opening time, though there will in-evitably be a queue. A visit to the information desk will help in planning the museum tour, which, given the sheer size of the building and the number of its galleries, will be repaid by a little forethought.

The British Museum was founded in 1753. In that year the physician Sir Hans Sloane died, leaving his asto-nishing collection of 80,000 objects to the nation. He demanded a suitable building, and a substantial payment to his heirs. A public lottery was held to raise the necessary funds, and free public access to the museum has been a cornerstone of its philosophy ever since – a great tradition for a great museum.

A statue of Sloane by John Michael Rysbraek (on loan from Chelsea Physic Garden) casts a benevolent, if rather weather-worn gaze over the museum visitors from a corner of the entrance hall. Sloane's collection was not only extensive but universal in scope. It included plants, fossils, pathological specimens, antiquities, prints, draw-ings, coins, medals, and books. This approach of gathering world culture is typified by the British Museum today. It is a celebration of human knowledge and achievement, with collections that have grown at an astonishing pace. There is a cool, stately feel to the major galleries of the museum, where it is the objects themselves that are always dramatised. An object might be mag-nificent in size, like the reconstructed façade of the Nereid monument, built as a tomb to one of the rulers of Xanthos around 400 BC; or it might be

be joined by a large crowd of fellow visitors. With over four million people going to the British Museum every year, this is one of Britain's premier tourist attractions.

It is worth getting into the museum

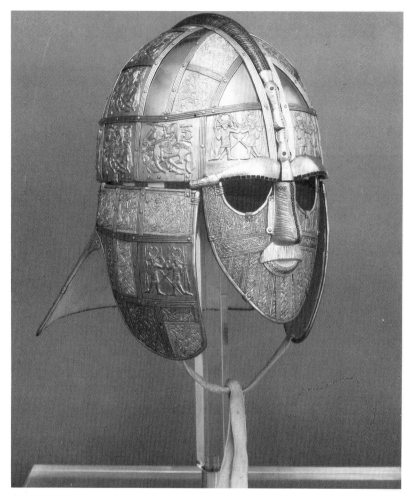

Replica of the helmet found at Sutton Hoo (made using electrotypes of excavated fragments)

Map of Elizabethan Exeter by John Hooker, 1587 (The British Library)

One of the most pleasurable galleries is devoted to the collection of clocks and watches. The slow and somehow graceful ticking of rare medieval clocks forms the back-drop to a gallery devoted to the development of mechanical time-keeping in Europe from the Middle Ages onwards. At the centre of the gallery is an extraordinarily elaborate ship-clock, or 'nef'. This is an automaton clock made for Emperor Rudolf II in Prague around 1580. It was designed to pitch and roll on the table, an organ playing a fanfare as the hours were struck, and the gun in the bowsprit fired. It is an extravagant aristocratic fancy, humorous and highly mannered.

Throughout the museum there are contrasts in scale and methods of display. Some galleries have a scholarly and old-fashioned air, such as Room 68, with its serried ranks of Etruscan bronze mirrors, Greek terracottas, and pottery lamps. Yet the following room shows a more public-spirited approach, giving life in Ancient Greece and Rome more of a human context by relating the objects to displays that describe customs and beliefs.

This contextual approach is also found in the popular series of mummies and mummy cases in the Egyptian rooms, displayed alongside the mummies of the sacred animals that were thought to be earthly manifestations of Egyptian gods. On the ground floor, the great display of columns, statues, and sarcophagi in the Egyptian Sculpture Gallery makes it one of the most visually stunning museum spaces anywhere in Britain. The dimly-lit side galleries recreate something of the

perfect in miniature, like the lovely 10th century walrus-ivory carving of the Baptism of Christ, displayed with the Trewhiddle Hoard from Cornwall.

There are marvels throughout the museum. The Roman mosaic from Hinton St Mary in Dorset, discovered in 1963, is 'undoubtedly one of the most outstanding Christian remains from Roman Britain', even the Roman world. Its quiet, and almost serene beauty contrasts with the adjoining display of Lindow Man. This is the astonishingly well-preserved upper half of a Briton who may have been slaughtered by druids. The agonised scream of death is caught for ever in his

expression. It is an eerie insight into a violent part of British life over 2000 years ago. This is a popular exhibit, partly because of its location close to the main entrance of the museum. The further the visitor reaches along the corridors and rooms of the museum, the easier it becomes to linger in front of less crowded cases. This is true of parts of the fine Early Medieval Room, which contains the 7th century finds from the Anglo-Saxon burial ship at Sutton Hoo. The famous Lewis chessmen, of 12th century Scandinavian work, are displayed with other notable antiquities from the Gothic and Byzantine periods in an adjacent gallery.

atmosphere of entering an Egyptian tomb.

The renowned sculptures from the Parthenon (removed from Athens by Lord Elgin at the beginning of the 19th century) are displayed in a light and elegant gallery. Equally famous is the Portland vase, on display in the first Roman room. This blue and white glass jar has scenes thought by many to illustrate the story of Peleus and Thetis, and owes its name to the Duchess of Portland, who acquired it in 1785.

The British Museum is a great living monument to learning and scholarship. It is unique by virtue of its size, status and situation, with collections of worldwide importance. The museum is authoritative, and yet quintessentially British in its mood of reticent magnificence.

Also housed in the British Museum are the exhibition galleries of the British Library. These display illuminated manuscripts, historical manuscripts and books, and notable maps from the British Library's collections, which include such treasures as the Magna Carta, and Shakespeare's first Folio.

Engraving of Bruce Castle in the 1680s

Bruce Castle Museum

Lordship Lane, London N17 8NU
01-808 8772
⊖ Wood Green ⇌ Bruce Grove
Open daily. ◼
♿ **X G**: no wheelchair access to first floor.
🚹 & 🚻 must book in advance.

Many museum buildings reputedly have ghosts. Bruce Castle has a more tragic one than most. A local paper, the *Tottenham and Edmonton Advertiser*, reported this gloomy 17th century legend in March 1858. It concerns one Lord Coleraine, resident at Bruce Castle, who 'married a beautiful lady and while she was yet in her youth had been siezed with a violent hatred against her . . . He first confined her to the upper part of the house and subsequently still more closely to the little rooms of the clock turret . . . the lady one night succeeded in forcing her way out and flung herself with child in arms from the parapet. The wild despairing shriek aroused the household only to find her and her infant in death's clutches below. Every year as the fearful night

Emperor Rudolf II's Ship-Clock, probably made by Hans Schlottheim, c. 1580–1600

comes round (it is in November) the wild form can be seen as she stood on the fatal parapet, and her despairing cry is heard floating away on the autumnal blast.'

This sounds like a good rewriting of legend into Victorian melodrama, as well as an account of the most diabolical patriarchal behaviour. Legend suits the Bruce Castle Museum, since the history of the building and its locality is still unclear. Bruce Castle is known to have been the manor house of Tottenham, held by King David of Scotland in 1124, and other members of the Scottish Royal Family, including Robert the Bruce. Today's building, and the adjoining tower, dates back in part to the 16th century, though much of it is of 18th-century construction. The postal reformer (and inventor of the penny post) Rowland Hill purchased the building for use as a highly successful school; it was acquired eventually by the local authority, and opened as a museum in 1906. The surrounding grounds were used, like now, as a public park.

Today, the museum is administered by the London Borough of Haringey, and is devoted to telling the complicated and rich history of the building, and the no-less rich history of the local community.

The introductory display, 'Changing Times', gives a clear and very well-illustrated account of past and present life in the borough, with detailed narrative panels covering themes such as employment, travel, and education. A picture of the essential contribution of ordinary lives to the history of the community is built up, especially through the fine photographs of local residents and workers.

A boy standing beside a 250kg German bomb during World War II

Clearly the museum is going through a transitional phase, as it redefines its analysis of the needs of local residents and visitors. New galleries are being developed, and the most recent displays are particularly successful. The upstairs room considers the theme of 'Riches of the East' with a display telling the borough's link with the East Indies trade. A reconstruction of an English drawing room belonging to a wealthy family of the 1830s makes the point that many items of furniture and decorative arts were imported from India or China. Even when they were made in this country, the influence of eastern cultures was profound. There is a good display of intricate ornamental Biridiware (traditional Indian metalwork), but the highlight of

Detail of the first known action photograph of Spurs, 1896

the display is the Indian Room, richly adorned with Indian rugs, cloth hangings, and household equipment, and presided over by the costumed figure of a seated merchant. A comparative study is made by an area furnished with Indian goods influenced by European styles and tastes – printed cotton cloths or a Bombay chair. These colourful historical cross-links make a sympathetic point about the valuable contribution of eastern culture to life in this part of London.

A recently-opened gallery on the upper floor describes the story of postal history, using an important collection on loan from the Union of Communication Workers. The collection stresses the vital importance of the history of communications in Britain and worldwide with a range of material, varying from a colourful and dramatic display of advertising posters to a Victorian pillar box.

Bruce Castle Museum even boasts a museum within the museum. On the first floor is the collection belonging to the Middlesex Regiment, which describes through costume, drums, medals, and other militaria the long history of the regiment known as the 'Die Hards'.

The Charles Darwin Memorial Museum

Down House, Downe, Kent BR6 7JT
(0689) 59119
⇌ Bromley South (about 6 miles away), Orpington (also some distance)
Closed in February, and on Mondays and Fridays. 🯀 ♿ X G
🚻 & ♿ must book in advance.

This is the London museum that feels least like a museum in London. If reached by public transport, the journey will be by a small country bus service from Bromley, which runs through delightful 'Kent' countryside, followed by a ten-minute walk along the sort of lane where the cottages have real cottage gardens, and houses have first-generation Morris Minors parked in their drives.

However much the Charles Darwin Museum looks to Kent (and feels part of it), the museum is situated in the London Borough of Bromley, though it is administered by the Royal College of Surgeons of England as a permanent memorial to the great naturalist, Charles Darwin, and his illustrious family.

Charles Darwin

Down House was Darwin's home for forty influential years from 1842 to 1882. The museum retains a domestic feel, with spacious rooms full of Victorian period pieces (side tables loaded with ornamental stags; a great display cabinet full of stuffed birds and butterflies). Those rooms open to the public are all on the ground floor, and include a gallery devoted to very detailed (and rather long-winded) notes on evolution, and authentically-displayed rooms with Darwin memorabilia.

Charles Darwin moved with his family in 1842 to Down House, Downe – then as now a small village with a feeling of remoteness from the centre of London. Many of Darwin's major scientific publications were produced during his long and contented stay in this house, including *On the Origin of Species by Means of Natural Selection*, and *Descent of Man* (1871). The Old Study has been retained in the house as Darwin would have remembered it, with many original furnishings, and Darwin's own books around the room. It has a gentle, scholarly atmosphere, befitting the character of a man who was known to be an engaging personality, never allowing his great intellect to overcrowd or dominate a relationship. His family knew him as someone with a manner often 'bright and animated . . . His laugh was a free and sounding

The voyage of HMS 'Beagle' to the Galapagos Islands

peal, like that of a man who gives himself sympathetically and with enjoyment to the person and thing which have amused him.'

The displays at Down House tell as much about the works of a major scientist as they do about living in a wealthy Victorian house (albeit that of an international celebrity). Rooms such as the Drawing Room (added to the house in 1858) are shown as closely as possible to their appearance in Darwin's lifetime, and in the Drawing Room are the family's grand piano, chairs, and bureau. The Charles Darwin Room was used as a Dining Room, and has displays relating to Darwin's voyage on board HMS 'Beagle' to the Galapagos Islands, where he thought out much of his original theory of evolution. The most important item here is the original manuscript of Darwin's Journal from 1831–36. Darwin was the official unpaid naturalist on the 'Beagle' voyage to South America.

Opposite this room, with its views across the attractive garden, is the Erasmus Darwin Room, used ultimately as a billiard room. It is now devoted to the life and work of Erasmus Darwin, Charles's grandfather

(1731–1802), regarded as one of the finest doctors of his generation, and known also as an influential literary figure, and an inventor. Notable among the displays that reflect his wide and eclectic interests is a group of oil paintings by Darwin's friend, Joseph Wright of Derby, including a dramatic self-portrait.

A visit to Down House should also include a trip around the gardens, which remain mostly as Darwin would have recognised. Darwin did most of his thinking on a regular walk from the back of the house to the Sandwalk Wood – planted with wild cherries and birches – and back (about one mile). Also in the garden is the Worm Stone: Darwin used this to note the time worms took to undermine objects placed in the soil, measured by an instrument on display in the Charles Darwin Room. The route of his walk is shown in the house and the guidebook, which also describes in some detail the context of Darwin's work, and the history of Down House itself, as well as providing a useful listing of objects on display. While there, it is worth a detour to the 13th century church of St Mary the Virgin in the village of Down.

Charles Darwin's study

Church Farm House Museum

Greyhound Hill, Hendon, London
NW4 4JR   01-203 0130
⊖ Hendon Central ⇌ Hendon
(some distance)
Closed Tuesday afternoons and
Sunday mornings. 🇫 🅿 ♿ S G
♿ & ♿ phone in advance.

The approach to Church Farm House Museum is through a piece of 'Country London'. A 'village pub', the parish church of Hendon St Mary, and even a 'Rose Cottage', stand close together beside the handsome museum, itself built during the reign of Charles II. There is a feeling of comfortable antiquity here, despite the fact that the museum is surrounded by the suburban sprawl typical of north London.

Church Farm House Museum is probably the oldest surviving house in the parish of Hendon. The main part of the building dates to the early and middle 17th century, though there are later additions, like the entrance porch. Three farms are known to have been located in this area, and an 18th century sale notice describes the building as 'an extraordinarily good Brick and Tiled House sash'd with two Barns boarded and tiled, a good Stable, Cowhouse, Woodhouse, Yard and Garden, and a Carthouse or Hayhouse all in good Repair.' Today, the house and garden survive – the garden one of the most attractive and pleasant surrounding any small museum in London.

The building has been altered throughout its long domestic history. Originally a rectangular structure with three rooms on the ground floor, Church Farm House developed from an earlier type of Hall house. Some original wooden panelling survives (though moved in the restoration of the house from the bedrooms to the central room on the ground floor), and the roof has been relaid to its original appearance using a thin thatch beneath hand-made tiles, fixed by oak pegs.

The outstanding feature in the house, and the room at the centre of its

Church Farm House, the Kitchen, c. 1820

domestic activities, is the farm kitchen, which retains the huge original fireplace and oak beam over the fire recess. Some stone paving is original, too, and minute traces of cow-dung have been found in the interior of the fireplace – the material with which it would originally have been lined.

The kitchen is used for the museum's permanent display of 18th and 19th century domestic equipment, an impressive array that indicates some radical changes in eating and cooking habits. Accounts of maids in middle-class houses, even as late as the 1920s, reveal the drudgery and sheer physical hard work involved in running a house. This would have included cleaning grates and laying fires at 6.30 in the morning, and sweeping, dusting, preparing meals, cleaning silver and brass, and trimming lamps right through until late evening. The bellows, cast iron kettles, and sad irons on display reflect this range of domestic tasks, and the functions of some of the more unfamiliar items, such as sugar cutters and fly catchers, are described in an accompanying leaflet.

The other small rooms in this quiet

Front view

and charming museum are used for a wide variety of temporary exhibitions. Some of these have been concerned with domestic themes, others have looked at the development of suburban housing, or similar local history topics. A complementary picture of life in the London Borough of Barnet is provided by the local history society at *Barnet Museum*. This small museum has a good collection, varying from archaeological material to a surprisingly good costume collection, and including some locally-made scientific instruments, and photographs and maps.

Commonwealth Institute

Kensington High Street, London
W8 6NQ   01-603 4535
⊖ High Street Kensington, Earls
Court
Closed Sunday mornings. 🄵 🖭 🅿
♿ W G: some problems for
wheelchairs; detailed access leaflet
available.
🚼 & 🚻 contact Education Centre
in advance; for talks or guided
tours contact Public Relations and
Marketing Office. ◎

The Commonwealth Institute makes
light of the challenge of making the
idea of Commonwealth not only interesting but relevant. At a time when
the notion and practice of the British
Empire (from which the modern Commonwealth has grown) is viewed with
suspicion and distrust, this is a challenge that would have tested anyone's
ingenuity. The Commonwealth Institute is a highly effective way of presenting the positive ideals of Commonwealth countries, which have made formal commitments to international
peace, equal rights, and opposition to
colonial domination and racial oppres-
sion. The political difficulties of
achieving these global ambitions, as far
as the issue of Apartheid is concerned,
shows that the notion of Commonwealth can be threatened almost to
breaking point. The Institute itself
makes an unambiguous statement about its intention, since the withdrawal
of South Africa from the Commonwealth in 1961, to be 'at the forefront
of the fight against Apartheid'.

The Commonwealth Institute is the
cultural centre for the forty-eight
member countries. Over forty permanent displays, organised by Commonwealth countries, give an insight into
their diverse cultures and lifestyles. In
addition, there is a lively programme of
temporary exhibitions, highly regarded
for being innovative and spectacular,
and there are popular performing arts
events to give even more variety to the
cultural experience.

Exterior view of the Commonwealth Institute

The Institute's building is a distinctive feature in its own right. Set back
from the bustle of Kensington High
Street, the flags of member nations
provide the building with a colourful
forefront. It was constructed between
1960 and 1962, with an extraordinary
five-peaked roof, clad in green copper.
The interior of the Institute manages
to be both friendly and magnificent at
the same time. From the central dais of
the great hall the visitor is surrounded
by the permanent displays of member
countries, and stands, suitably enough,
as part of, and at the middle of, the
Commonwealth. The open-plan
arrangement of galleries on three
floors makes it particularly easy to plan
a tour, since the visitor will always be
able to see across to the other galleries.

A helpful 'passport' is available from
the Institute's excellent shop, to assist
in planning a route around the galleries. The ground floor contains a sort of
Cook's tour of countries, from Canada
to India, and Papua New Guinea to
New Zealand. The middle floor fo-
cuses on the African nations of the
Commonwealth. It begins with an exhibition, 'Africa in History', which
vividly describes Africa's life and culture before foreign settlement. The top
floor contains displays from the Carib-
bean, South-East Asia, and parts of
Europe like the Channel Islands and
the Isle of Man.

The displays are all presented in a
colourful and dynamic way through the
use of models, dioramas, photographs,
plants, fabrics, and reconstructions, as
well as original artefacts. There are
some stunning exhibits: the Nigerian

Children celebrating Trinidad Carnival

Courtauld Institute Galleries

Woburn Square, London WC1H OAA (to 30 July 1989, after which moving to **Somerset House***, where scheduled to open Nov. 1989; phone for details 01-580 1015/636 2095)*

▴ Goodge Street, Russell Square

⇋ Euston

Open daily. 🖺

♿ X: steps to main entrance, but help can be arranged if notice given.

🚻 & 🚺 arrange by phone giving one week's notice.

The Courtauld Institute of Art (part of the University of London) was founded in 1931 to provide teaching, research and conservation facilities in art that today have an internationally-famous reputation. Allied to the Institute is an equally renowned collection of paintings, drawings and works of decorative art, which has until now been on display in an upper-floor gallery in Woburn Square, but is moving to new premises at Somerset House.

The Courtauld Collections have developed from the gifts and bequests of Samuel Courtauld, the founder of the Institute, whose intention was to provide the University of London with an Institute of Art, and to use his magnificent collection for research and teaching. Courtauld had collected an outstanding series of Impressionist and

Gagalo stilt dancer, perched high above the visitor, or the skilfully-made and highly-detailed bronze models of Ganesh, the god of fortune from India, are especially memorable. Throughout the Institute photographs and information panels stress the human element

Gagalo stiltman from West Africa (a model is featured in the Africa galleries)

to each country's story, and there are also good audio-visual programmes. These add to the noise, and to the eventful atmosphere that is one of the endearing characteristics of the Institute.

Throughout the main exhibition, the pavilion devoted to each country gives a clear idea of its achievements, history, industry, and culture. There are also two temporary exhibition galleries, which develop specific themes or subjects in the visual arts. The main gallery hosts impressive art exhibitions, and the smaller Bhownagree Gallery is often used as a space for first-time shows by young Commonwealth artists.

When the Commonwealth Institute was opened to the public in this new building in 1962, there were only fifteen independent Commonwealth states. The rapid changes in the Commonwealth itself are reflected in the Institute's own exciting plans for rebuilding and redevelopment. This will emphasise its place as a pioneering cultural centre, and one of the most enjoyable and rewarding museums in London.

Vanessa Bell, A Conversation, *1913 (Fry Collection)*

Edouard Manet, A Bar at the Folies-Bergère, *1881–82 (Courtauld Collection)*

Post-Impressionist paintings, and these are central to the galleries' displays. There have been many important additions to these fine art works, from a range of artistic periods.

There are 20th century works of art by the Bloomsbury Group and the Omega Workshops, along with Roger Fry's collection of paintings. Old Master and Italian Renaissance paintings were bequeathed by Viscount Lee of Fareham in 1947, and Mark Gambier-Parry in 1966; the latter bequest is also notable for the inclusion of medieval ivories and enamels, Italian glass, Islamic metalwork, and Italian maiolica pottery.

To add to the quality and variety of these major collections, further outstanding gifts have been made, like that of Turner watercolours (a gift from the Courtauld family in memory of Sir Stephen Courtauld), and the superb Princes Gate Collection of Old Master Paintings and Drawings, bequeathed by Count Antoine Seilern, with a particularly fine and large group of oil paintings by Rubens.

The Courtauld Institute Galleries display one of the finest collections of paintings, watercolours and drawings in London, with some renowned and well-loved works on show. Gauguin's

oil painting, 'Nevermore', was once owned by the composer Delius, and has a sombre, melancholic mood. His 'Te Rerioa' (meaning day-dreaming) is another of Gauguin's painting from Tahiti (colour plate p.?). Other notable works from the Courtauld collection include Manet's 'Le Déjeuner sur l'Herbe', and his last work, the famous 'Bar at the Folies-Bergère'.

The Gambier-Parry bequest includes some fine 15th century sculpture, alongside religious paintings, and there is a commanding biblical work by Pieter Bruegel the Elder in the Princes Gate Collection – the 'Landscape with

Rembrandt van Rijn, A Quack addressing a Crowd at a Fair *(Princes Gate Collection)*

the Flight into Egypt'. The great sequence of oils by Rubens includes sketches for altarpieces, and Old and New Testament scenes. There are also important drawings in the Princes Gate Collection, including works by Michelangelo, Rembrandt, and Leonardo de Vinci. The Courtauld Institute's principal group of drawings is the large Witt Collection, which embraces a rich variety of Dutch, Flemish, Italian, French, German, and British drawings.

The Courtauld Institute's remarkable art collection has, for some time, outgrown its current location at Woburn Square, and both the Institute and Galleries will be moving to prestigious new premises at Somerset House, scheduled to open to the public at the end of 1989. The Somerset House Act of 1984 established a lease between the Government and the University of London, allowing the Galleries to move into the historic Fine Rooms at Somerset House. This building takes its name from the former royal palace of Somerset House (built by Edward, Duke of Somerset, the Lord Protector, and forfeited to the Crown after his execution in 1552), which once stood on this site. The present Somerset House was built in the neo-classical style by the Royal Architect, Sir William Chambers, between 1776 and 1780, as government offices, and to house the Royal Academy, Royal Society, and Society of Antiquaries. These learned societies occupied a suite of rooms known as the Fine Rooms, which were richly decorated with elaborate plasterwork and paintings. The Great Room was used for Royal Academy exhibitions from 1780 to 1836. When the societies moved to new premises in Piccadilly, they took with them Benjamin West's pictures, and most of those by Angelica Kauffmann; the Fine Rooms were then occupied by government offices. Some decorations by Angelica Kauffman and by Cipriani, however, remain to this day at Somerset House. The Fine Rooms will be a fittingly splendid location for the Courtauld Institute's superlative collection of fine and decorative arts.

The Cutty Sark

King William Walk, Greenwich,
London SE10 9HT   01-858 3445/
853 3589
⊖ New Cross (some distance)
⇌ Greenwich. Docklands
Light Railway: Island Gardens.
Open daily. ⚑ Free coach park
alongside ship.
♿ **S**: wheelchair access to tween
deck, stair lift to lower hold where
wheelchairs available.
🚻 & 🍴 book in advance by phone,
minimum 15 people.

The 'Cutty Sark', the last surviving and most famous sailing tea clipper, is a great symbol of maritime history set in a significant corner of maritime England, beside the river Thames at Greenwich. Within easy walking distance lie Sir Francis Chichester's tiny yacht, 'Gypsy Moth IV' (used on his solo journey around the world), the Royal Naval College, and the **National Maritime Museum**, all of which combine to make a rewarding and nautical day trip.

The 'Cutty Sark' is an impressive and dignified sight in dry dock, whether the approach is by foot or by boat, arriving at Greenwich Pier. The great masts and complex rigging tower high above the visitor, giving some idea of what the great ship must have looked like at sea, with three-quarters of an acre of sail billowing out as the 'Cutty Sark' sped forward at seventeen knots.

A major feature of the sailing calendar in the 19th century was the annual China Tea Race. The winner was awarded 'the blue riband of the sea', gaining much prestige and fame, profit to the ship's owner, and a bonus to the captain. The 'Cutty Sark' was built specifically to win this great contest for the owner, 'Jock' Willis. The ship was launched from the Old Woodyard at Dumbarton, Scotland, in 1869, and started work as a tea clipper. However, this was an unprofitable business from the outset, since after the opening of the Suez Canal the tea trade went to the quicker steam ships, which were not so dependent on weather condi-

The Cutty Sark *at Greenwich*

tions. The 'Cutty Sark' only made eight voyages in the tea trade, and on the second trip, from Shanghai to England in 1871, won lasting fame by completing the fastest voyage of 107 days. The ship continued to carry miscellaneous cargoes, before regularly taking wool cargoes in the 1880s and 1890s from Australia to England. After this, the 'Cutty Sark' was sold to a Portuguese Company, and sailed as the 'Ferreira'. Following a spell as a training ship in Falmouth and at Greenhithe on the Thames (1922–54), it was given to the Cutty Sark Society, which in partnership with the Maritime Trust displays a wide range of historic vessels from Dundee to Portsmouth. The 'Cutty Sark' has been on public

display at Greenwich since 1957, and is one of Britain's best-known tourist attractions. The ship has been carefully restored to as original a condition as possible, to its heyday in the 1870s when the ship was a first-rate tea clipper, and it is shown as if docked between voyages in its home port of London.

The 'Cutty Sark' takes its name from a character in the poem, 'Tam o'Shanter', by Robert Burns, which tells the story of Tam, a drunken farmer, who sees the Devil dancing with a group of witches on the journey home, riding on his grey mare. One of the witches, Nannie, wears a short shirt of Paisley linen, known as a Cutty Sark. The ship's figurehead shows Nannie

Tam o'Shanter, *with the witch in her 'Cutty Sark' (short linen shirt)*

The Dickens House Museum

48 Doughty Street, London WC1N 2LF   01-405 2127
⊖ Chancery Lane, Holborn, Kings Cross, Russell Square
⇌ Kings Cross
Closed Sundays. ▣
& S G: steps to first floor.
⋈ & ⋔ by arrangement with Curator.

The popularity of 'personality' museums continues to grow, and there are very many of them in London, from the new *Florence Nightingale Museum* to the **Freud Museum**. This must have something to do with the particular claim of the authentic: objects really used by famous people, houses really lived in by household names.

The Dickens House Museum is no exception. The rooms of the late 18th century house are full of Dickensiana, from serious portraits and illustrations, to the small objects that patterned a gregarious and abundant lifestyle. Here are things that are stately (marble busts of the author), pertinent (the quill pens used to write the great novels), or even faintly odd (fragments of curtains once owned by Dickens). The museum is both a tribute to the life and work of the famous author, and a passport to the products of the 'Dickens Industry' – the ceramic figures of

grasping the tail of the farmer's horse, and the story is explained in detail in the exhibition on the upper cargo deck.

This well-written display is also concerned with the origins of the ship and its complex history, and is supported by ship models and paintings. Below, in the lower hold (which used to carry most of the ship's cargo), is a colourful and intriguing display of merchant-ship figureheads from the Long John Silver Collection, created by Captain John Cumbers. The figureheads are fine examples of 19th century wood-carving and painting, and give a haunting reminder of long-lost ships, some of which, like the barque 'Maude' (which became an isolation hulk at Plymouth), or the 'Garibaldi' (wrecked off the Orkney Islands) came to tragic or desolate fates.

The 'Cutty Sark' may look a commanding sight from dry land, but life on board ship during the ninety-day journey from Australia must have meant many severe hardships for the crew. There are excellent reconstructions of living quarters on board, from the officers' rooms to the tiny galley and carpenter's shop. There is a

marked contrast between the richly-panelled saloon, with its highly-polished teak and bird's-eye-maple walls, ornately laid out with silver and cut glass for the officers' dinner, and the primitive and cramped quarters where the sailors slept.

The 'Cutty Sark' is a famous reminder of great days from the sailing era, with a collection that not only brings to life the triumphs of maritime history, but also gives a glimpse into the gruelling living conditions of a working, commercial ship.

Captain Richard Woodget, the most famous master of the 'Cutty Sark', 1924

The Drawing Room, Dickens House

Charles Dickens's last reading

characters from his books, the leather-bound editions, and the stills from films and television series.

All of these miscellaneous objects continue to give life to the Dickens legend. Some merely add a note of fantasy, such as the quaint figure of Charles Dickens manufactured in sugar as a cake decoration. Others, such as the grill in the basement, reputedly from the Marshalsea Prison (where Dicken's father served a three-month prison term for debt), pay heed to the grim and poverty-sticken lives depicted by Dickens in his great stories of London's low life. Altogether there is a feeling of carefully interpreted clutter in the house, with the objects described – fittingly enough, in a writer's house – on ink-written information labels.

The Dickens House Museum is an important building in its own right. Although it was Dickens's home for only about three years (1837–39), he lived here at a critical stage in his career, when he was just building on an early and yet substantial reputation as an author. Dickens wrote a number of influential works at Doughty Street, finishing *Pickwick Papers*, writing most of *Oliver Twist* and *Nicholas Nickleby*,

and starting *Barnaby Rudge*. But the house is not only important for its place in literary history: it had a tragic role to play in Dickens's emotional life. Dickens was particularly fond of Mary Hogarth, his young sister-in-law, a frequent visitor to Doughty Street. On her last visit, Mary had a quite unexpected heart attack, dying in Dickens's arms in her bedroom (on view in the museum). The shock of this incident affected Dickens for a long time, and is recalled in the pathetic death scene of Little Nell in *The Old Curiosity Shop*.

The collection in the museum contains objects from all periods of Dickens's life and not just the years he spent with his wife and young family here. In the study on the first floor, for example, is Dickens's desk from Gad's Hill Place, Rochester, which he used at the end of his life, and the table on which he wrote *The Mystery of Edwin Drood* the day before his death. In the Morning Room there is a reminder of Dickens's youthful employment as a lawyer's clerk in Gray's Inn – the desk that he worked at, complete with its graffiti.

The Drawing Room, the front room on the first floor, is a particularly important shrine for the many Dickens students and enthusiasts who make the pilgrimage to Doughty Street. It is here that a careful programme of restoration has taken place in an effort to return the room to a decorative scheme that Dickens himself would have recognised immediately. The room has been restored to the appearance of 1839, just before Dickens left Doughty Street. Some of the furniture in the Drawing Room belonged to Dickens, and the colour scheme of the walls and woodwork has been identified through paint scrapings. The carpet is modern, though similar to one in an illustration by George Cruickshank for *Oliver Twist*, so it has a genuine air of authenticity, and correct period feel.

This room, as well as the Dining Room on the ground floor, played host regularly to the friendly and garrulous company kept by the author and his family. Dickens held regular dinner parties for his artistic and literary friends – people such as the illustrators

George Cruickshank and H. K. Browne ('Phiz'), or publishing colleagues and actors. The Still Room, Wash House, and Wine Cellar in the basement remain to remind us of the business involved in running the domestic affairs of a large house, and have been restored to conditions similar to those that Dickens would have known.

The museum is host to one specific and large collection of Dickensiana, displayed in Dickens's bedroom and Dressing Room, the so-called Suzannet Rooms. This material was collected by the Comte Alain de Suzannet from 1920, and includes important documentary pieces such as the earliest portrait of Dickens (a miniature by his aunt of 1830), manuscripts, and original editions. The collection also includes material relating to Dickens's friends and colleagues, and a particularly impressive group of original drawings for the novels. The Dressing Room displays some of Dickens's personalised volumes, which he used for his famous series of public reading performances; here too is the desk, covered with velvet, that Dickens used on these extensive tours across Britain and America.

Charles Dickens and his daughters in the grounds of Gads Hill Place, Rochester

Dulwich Picture Gallery

College Road, London SE21 7BG
01-693 5254
Recorded information   01-693 8000
⇄ West Dulwich, North Dulwich
Closed Mondays. ▣ ♿ X
♨ & ♥ book 2 weeks in advance;
guided tours available for parties
of 16 or more by arrangement with
Keeper. ◎

In 1844 the famous Victorian art critic,
John Ruskin, wrote in his diary after a
visit to the Dulwich Picture Gallery:
'Thought the pictures worse than ever;
came away encouragingly disgusted.'
Ruskin may have been annoyed by
what he saw: today's visitor will be
delighted, and more than likely to
agree with the opinion of a *Guardian*
writer that here is 'London's most
perfect art gallery'.

A number of factors come together
to inspire this lyrical praise, which has
been repeated by many of the famous
visitors to the Gallery (Dickens and
Tennyson included), or those artists
who come to copy from the great collection of paintings. The Gallery has a
notable history: it is the oldest public
art gallery in England, opening in
1817. It is beautifully situated, and was
commissioned as a purpose-built gallery from the famous architect, Sir
John Soane (see **Sir John Soane's
Museum** and **Pitshanger Manor
Museum**).

Soane's architecture for the Gallery
emphasised clear, airy spaces, lit from
above by fine skylights. It is a design
that has had many imitators, and one
that is seen to perfection at Dulwich.
The nucleus of the collection of paintings (the majority of which are on
permanent display) was brought
together by a French dealer, Noel Desenfans, in the 1790s, while attempting
to create a national gallery for the last
King of Poland. Desenfans concentrated on the great works of the 17th
and 18th centuries, buying in particular celebrated paintings by Dutch and
Flemish artists, such as Rembrandt,

Paul Sandby, Desenfans *(right)* and
Bourgeois *(left)*

Rubens, Hobbema and Cuyp. Desenfans's plans to create a gallery in Poland were dashed by the King's abdica-
tion. The British government rejected
Desenfans's suggestion that the state
should buy the collection to form a new
national gallery. Eventually, with the
help of his friend Francis Bourgeois,
400 paintings were exhibited to the
public at Dulwich, close to the centre
of London. Bourgeois was keen to
place the collection in Dulwich for its
country location. There is still an
atmosphere of tranquil rural charm as
one approaches the original (and in its
day controversial) building, surrounded by fields and parks, next to
the 17th century buildings of Dulwich
College. Bourgeois is known, in fact, to
have believed that the fresh country air
would be of benefit to the pictures, and
the courteous response he received
from the Governors of the College
settled his mind as to the location.

Soane created a harmonious and
elegant interior, with fine vistas
through the galleries. There is also a
mausoleum for the benefactors, which
contains a temple-like antechamber,
and a sepulchre building bathed in an
eery amber light, which shows the sarcophagi of Bourgeois, and of Desenfans and his wife, in a suitably contem-
plative atmosphere.

The twelve galleries of the museum
contain the dense hang of paintings
that has always been a feature at Dulwich, supported by a choice collection
of French and English furniture, much

of it from the gift of Mrs Desenfans.
Highlights of the collection include a
number of works by Albert Cuyp in the
Dutch Italianate style, shown in Gallery VI. The small scale room, with its
cool green walls, is an ideal setting for
paintings like 'Road near a River', with
its tranquil, warm, golden daylight.
Lovers of works by Thomas Gainsborough will be delighted by the unique collection of nine portraits from
the Linley bequest, which includes one
of Gainsborough's most famous paintings, 'The Linley Sisters'. Also from
the bequest of Thomas Linley, the
18th century composer and musician,
is the portrait of his son, Samuel. It has
a spontaneous and informal quality,
and is reputed to have been painted by
Gainsborough in one sitting of less
than an hour.

Paintings by Rembrandt are among
the best known works in the collection,
and include 'Girl Leaning on a Stone
Pedestal' (1645), and the 'Portrait of a
Young Man' that is thought to be a
study of the artist's son, Titus.

Many of the best works in Dulwich's
collection – by Poussin, Tiepolo,
Murillo, Van Dyck and Canaletto –
were exhibited in a tour to American
museums in 1985 and 1986, and are
described in an extensive and well-

Dance at Dulwich

illustrated catalogue, *Collection for a King*, which charts the history of the Gallery and its building. The Gallery also originates its own temporary exhibitions, which are always well attended and highly regarded in the art world.

Thomas Gainsborough, The Linley Sisters, c. *1772*

Picture galleries have a reputation for being places only suitable for a few, and forbidding to the ordinary visitor. Dulwich Picture Gallery defies this label: it is welcoming, alive, and enjoyable. The Gallery has developed an important education programme, which is the envy of many British museums, and schools' concerts, dance, art-work, and storytelling form the basis of lively education work, designed to show the relevance of the historic paintings collection.

When Soane designed the mausoleum he included a domed lantern that was later used by Gilbert Scott in his classic 1924 design of the K2 telephone kiosk. The museum has recently installed one of these well-loved red telephone boxes within its grounds, with a two-minute talk on the history of the building. It is a spirited touch, typical of the verve and style that characterise the work of this enchanting museum.

Freud Museum

20 Maresfield Gardens, London NW3 5SX   01-435 2002
⊖ Finchley Road
Closed Mondays and Tuesdays. ▣
& **A** ground floor, **S** remaining floors, **G**.
♟ & ♟♟ book at least 48 hours in advance.

The Freud Museum in Hampstead is one of the most impressive and important new museums to open in London in recent years. It is situated in the house that became the home of Sigmund Freud, the founder of psychoanalysis.

Freud was eighty-two years old by the time he and his family came to their adopted country. He joined his son, Ernst, in London, writing to him just before his trip: 'two prospects keep me going in these grim times: to rejoin you and . . . to die . . . in freedom . . . compared to being liberated nothing is of any importance.' Freud had visited England in his youth, and he wrote to H.G. Wells attributing his long attachment to England to 'an intense wish phantasy to . . . become an Englishman'. Freud lived and worked in this house for one year before his death in 1939. His daughter, Anna, the celebrated child psychoanalyst, continued to live in the house until her death in 1982, by which time she had sold it to the charitable organisation, Sigmund Freud Archives, intending it to be converted into a permanent museum.

Thanks to the influence and financial support of friends and colleagues, Freud was able to rescue from Vienna his entire domestic and working environment, including his extraordinary collection of antiquities, his huge library and correspondence, and items of furniture, including the famous couch. His youngest son, Ernst, recreated his father's Viennese working environment

Freud's couch

at the Maresfield Gardens house with the help of photographs and the family housekeeper, so that Freud could resume work in a familiar setting.

The ground floor of the Freud Museum contains Freud's study exactly as it was in 1939. This room and the library were preserved by Anna Freud after her father's death as a memorial to him. On display is the famous analytic couch, covered with a colourful Turkish rug. Freud would listen to his patients as they rested on the couch, asking them to say whatever came into their minds without consciously selecting information. This method of free association became the basis of modern psychoanalysis. Freud was still working and seeing patients during his residence in Hampstead, and the palpable atmosphere of these two rooms remains. He would often point to antiquities from his collection in the study to illustrate a psychoanalytic point, and used the archaeologist's work of uncovering the layers of civilisations as a metaphor for describing the psychoanalytic process of penetrating the hidden layers of the unconscious. Freud was a very keen collector of antiquities, often visiting archaeological sites, although he bought most of his collections from Viennese dealers. He is said to have regarded collecting as a passion second only to his habit of smoking cigars – a habit that led to cancer of the jaw, from which he suffered during the last sixteen years of his life. His desk is crowded with Greek, Roman, Oriental, and Egyptian figures, and the walls are lined with Freud's library of books on subjects as diverse as psychology, art,

Egyptian funeral boat from Freud's collection of antiquities

Sigmund Freud

literature, archaeology, history, mythology, and anthropology.

There is an inevitable air of a time-warp about the study and library, a tribute to the meticulous reconstruction of the rooms. But this is a living museum, and the upper floor is used for interpretive displays, temporary exhibitions, and audio-visual displays. The Anna Freud room pays tribute to her life and work as a pioneer of child analysis, and also shows her enthusiasm for weaving and other crafts.

The Freud Museum tells a dramatic and important story in a quiet suburban road. There is little in the solid neo-Georgian façade of the house to prepare one for the rich and authentic Viennese consulting room inside – a memorable contrast of styles.

The museum is developing an exhibition programme to introduce visitors to Freud's contribution to our way of thinking about ourselves and our society, and to put the collections and domestic story into an appropriate historical context. The museum hosts courses and seminars on psychoanalytical themes, and material from Freud's library – as well as some unpublished material – is available to researchers. Guided tours of the house help to explain the Freud story in more detail, and archive films, including the Freud Home Movies, are also shown.

Geffrye Museum

Kingsland Road, London E2 8EA
01-739 9893; recorded information
01-739 8543; out of hours answering
service 01-739 9896
⊖ Liverpool Street, Old Street
⇌ Liverpool Street
Closed Mondays except Bank holidays. 🅵 ⬛ &♿ W
♨ & ♀♂ must book in advance. ◎
East End Furniture Archive.

The Geffyre Museum is a very important museum indeed, notable for the quality and interpretation of its collections, its well-researched temporary exhibitions, and an outstanding history of education work for schools in London and beyond.

The Museum takes its title from Sir Robert Geffrye (1613–1703/4), Lord Mayor of London in 1685 and Master of the Ironmongers Company, whose fortune was made through the slave trade. He left his estate to the Ironmongers for the purpose of building Almshouses for the poor, and this was fulfilled by 1715 through the construction of a graceful row of fourteen houses with a central chapel. In 1914, the buildings were converted into a museum devoted to the history of the furniture and cabinet-making trades

Thomas Dugdale, The Arrival of the Jarrow Marchers in London, *1936*

that surrounded the locality in the East End of London. The museum changed its emphasis and approach in 1939, under the influential curatorship of Marjorie Quennell, who created the series of room settings that lie at the heart of today's museum.

The Geffrye Museum adopts a chronological approach along its slender sequence of galleries to tell the changing history of the British front room from the 17th to the 20th centuries. The museum makes some telling statements about middle class life, and about how people reflected their cultural ideas and tastes through the decoration of their domestic interiors. This is as much a museum of the trades of furniture making as the history of design ideas, and the informative labels beside each room setting make these connections clearly and incisively. There is a definite sense of purpose to the interpretation. Each room setting has a different mood and character typical of its period, from the grace and decorum of the Early Georgian Room of a wealthy family, to the abundant clutter of the Mid-Victorian Room.

There is a small temporary exhibition area, which the museum devotes to themes relevant to its collections. Recent shows (such as 'The Things That Time Forgot', using objects lent by local people displayed beside objects from the museum) have been extremely popular. It is well worth reading the narrative panels in any show originated by the museum, for they are among the clearest and best-written of any museum in London.

John Piper, The Geffrye Museum in Autumn

The mid-Victorian room

The museum's education programme has also achieved success in making the difficult concepts of design, taste, and furniture history both accessible and enjoyable to many thousands of school parties. A visit to the Geffrye is cherished by countless London schoolchildren and adults.

One of the best known objects in the museum's collection is the famous Cabinet of Curiosities, bought by the Geffrye in 1979. It was made for the diarist and courtier, John Evelyn, in Paris in 1652. Evelyn was a scholar and collector, and like many learned antiquarians of the day, made a rich and varied collection of European, African, and West Indian objects of natural history and archaeology. The cabinet is shown with a typical range of material from other collections, such as stuffed animals, exotic shells, and minerals. It is a museum in miniature itself, and demonstrates the fascination for knowledge and quest for learning that continue to inform educational work at the Geffrye Museum today. Evelyn's cabinet is a perfect symbol for the museum, and is beautifully displayed in an authentically historical setting.

Other highlights are the Georgian

The 1930s suburban lounge

Street, displaying a range of shopfronts and street furniture from 18th century London, and the Mid-Victorian Room. The latter shows very clearly the radical effect that the mass-production of furniture and fabrics had on interior design. The room has a cluttered, rich atmosphere, with ornate dark wood furniture crammed into a small space, every surface used for ornaments, and the walls crowded with contemporary prints and paintings. Two upper rooms beside the exhibition hall are displayed with 1930s furniture, and there are plans for a 1950s room.

*1   Giovanna Baccelli by
Thomas Gainsborough,
first exhibited 1782. Tate
Gallery*

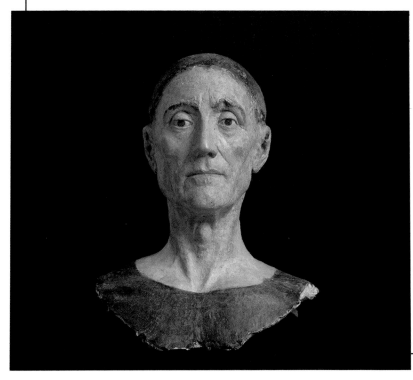

2 *Above*   *Reconstruction of John Carter and Son garage at Pentlepoir. Heritage Motor Museum.*

3 *Left*   *Head of the effigy of Henry VII. Westminster Abbey Museum.*

4 *Above*   *View looking up the main staircase in the Main Entrance Hall of the Clore Gallery. Tate Gallery.*

5 *Right*   *Indian sculpture of Usnisavijaya, Goddess of Holy Life. The Horniman Museum and Library.*

E X P L O R E
LONDON

WITH A LONDON TRANSPORT EXPLORER PASS

6 Opposite Poster designed for London Transport by Catherine Denvir, 1986. London Transport Museum.

7 Right View of the Dome area. Sir John Soane's Museum.

8 Below Exterior view. Royal Air Force Museum.

9 *Opposite* Boy Punk *by Candace Bahouth, 1985.*
Victoria and Albert Museum.

10 *Right* Longquan celadon temple vase, Yuan
dynasty, dated by inscription to 1327 AD. Percival
David Foundation of Chinese Art.

11 *Below* Lady's Court dress of about 1870.
Kensington Palace, Court Dress Collection and State
Apartments.

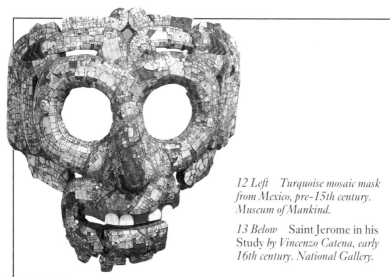

*12 Left   Turquoise mosaic mask
from Mexico, pre-15th century.
Museum of Mankind.*

*13 Below   Saint Jerome in his
Study by Vincenzo Catena, early
16th century. National Gallery.*

Geological Museum

(British Museum [Natural History])

Exhibition Road, London SW7 2DE
01-938 8765
⊖ South Kensington
Open daily. ⊠
♿ W G: parking space phone
01 938 9141.
♦♦ book in advance through
Education Department
(01 938 9049).

In 1839, Henry de la Beche (1796–1855) was engaged on a project for the Geological Society, funded by the British Government, to study the geology of Devon. His belief that the collection of minerals, rocks, and fossil specimens that would result from this task would also be of educational use led ultimately to the creation of a small museum in Whitehall. The collection grew rapidly (as museum collections do), new premises were found, and eventually the current building in South Kensington was purpose-built, and the Geological Museum opened in 1935.

The museum has developed since the days in the mid-19th century when specimens could only be studied 'by suitably qualified persons' into the popular and welcoming museum of today. The museum covers the themes of British regional geology, economic geology worldwide, and, more emphatically now, the whole subject of Earth Science. The roots of the Geological Museum in systematic collecting and recording, and in scholarly research and investigation, are shown most clearly in the first and second-floor

Model of a Trilobite (an animal known from fossil remains)

Crinoid Pentacrinites, *Jurassic period*

Cut and facetted piece of Beryl

galleries. These will interest the serious amateur and professional geologists, rather than the casual visitor. The explanatory labels require some knowledge of the subject, and the layout of the cases is typical of a study collection. On the second floor is the largest display of metalliferous ores and useful non-metallic minerals in existence. There is a bay devoted to building stones and marbles, which is of particular interest, and some colourful, fine British minerals. These specimens are worth looking at, since they have been selected for their perfect colouring and form.

On the first floor there is also a

gallery formally laid out with symmetrical groups of bays, this time containing material showing Britain's geology in detail. Rocks, fossils, and minerals are shown according to geological regions. A new gallery, devoted to the story of Britain's offshore oil and gas, is clearly and thoughtfully laid out in the modern style, using plenty of working exhibits. There are plans to replace the regional geology cases with exhibitions on the scenery and geological formations found throughout Britain.

The Geological Museum is really two museums in one: a scholarly survey backed up by a huge reference collection; and a more interactive and thematic display, which will appeal to the ordinary visitor as much as the serious student. The gallery, 'British Fossils', on the mezzanine floor, takes a more relaxed explanatory style, and introduces models, a video, and a large push-button map to encourage the visitor to get involved in the narrative. The display is based on the great collections built up over 150 years by the British Geological Survey, and loaned to the Geological Museum. It shows a systematic display of fossils according to geological age, and is an interpretative introduction to the subject of fos-

Museum of Practical Geology at Jermyn Street, 1875

sils, answering the basic questions of what they are, and where they can be found.

The permanent exhibition, 'Britain before Man', takes the results of new scientific research to tell the story of the development of Britain's early geological history. This is done through static displays, from the 'Dark Ages' of Pre-Cambrian time to the Ice Age. A projection theatre shows a helpful introductory programme, 'Britain from the Beginning'. The use of dioramas, paintings, and large models illuminates the technical information.

'Treasures of the Earth' is a display that shows how the Geological Museum deals with current and future applications of the earth's natural resources. It takes an up-beat approach to show which minerals are used in everyday products; a cut-away house forms a successful display, with push buttons enabling visitors to find out where the different materials taken from the earth have been used. A number of computer-operated data-banks encourage the visitor to ask further questions about the geology of the materials used in manufacture. This is a bright, informative, and 'user-friendly' gallery, which is well used,

especially by children, and completely different in feel from the upper two galleries of the museum.

'The Story of the Earth' was the first British Earth Sciences exhibition based on the new theory of plate techtonics. The entrance forms the centre-piece of the museum – a huge replica rock-face from the North–West Highlands of Scotland, towering above the visitor. It is one of the most dramatic 'ways in' to any museum exhibition in Britain. The visitor is immediately taken into a darkened gallery, which considers the story of deep space. Profound matters of time and space are emphasised here – time measured in millions of years, temperature in thousands of degrees centigrade. The sample of moonrock lent by NASA is 4,000 million years old, and it is possible to touch a sedimentary rock from Greenland, one of the oldest rocks on Earth. The sounds and motions of geology in action are also featured in this popular and dramatic exhibition. The visitor can watch a model of a volcanic eruption at the touch of a button, and feel the ominous earth-moving effect of a real earthquake (based on the terrible Alaskan earthquake of 1964).

The central hall of the Geological Museum contains its priceless collection of gem stones. The cases show natural crystals, as well as cut and carved stones. There are over 3000 of the most outstanding examples on display. Some of the most attractive items are the deep and vivid blue slabs of lapis lazuli from Afghanistan, and the multi-coloured opals from Mexico and Australia.

In the Demonstration Room at the Geological Museum

The Grange Museum of Community History

Neasden Lane, London NW10 1QB
01-908 7432
⊖ Neasden
Closed Sundays and Mondays.
🅵 🅿
♿ **G**: access to ground floor only (exhibition gallery, conservatory and garden);
first floor and toilets inaccessible.
🖾 & 🚻 must book in advance: contact Education Officer. Local history library and archive.

The Grange Museum stands unusually, and with an air of elegant defiance, in the middle of Neasden Roundabout in the London Borough of Brent. Defiance is an appropriate face for the building, which has been regularly threatened with demolition. It was purchased by the then Willesden Borough Council in 1962 to save it from that fate. A public enquiry eventually ensured the preservation of the property, though the pedestrian approach is now down a footbridge, from which the rush of traffic along the North Circular Road is clearly visible. The situation of the museum is a

Trade Union certificate, 1914

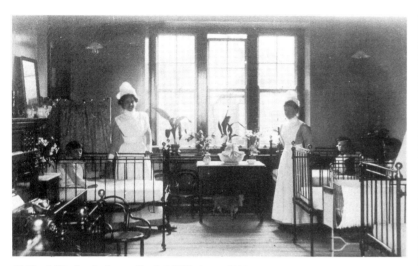

Children's Ward at the Cottage Hospital, Willesden, c. 1908

furniture) from the private collection of George Barham of Wembley.

The displays in this small yet appealing museum are well presented to cover themes of work, transport, leisure, and life in the borough. There are two authentic room settings – a Victorian parlour and a 1930s lounge – which gives a clear idea of the contrast in decorative styles, furniture, and social habits between the centuries. A complete Edwardian drapers' shop from Willesden High Street has been rebuilt in the museum.

This crowded and cosy museum is evidently popular with its visitors, especially school parties. A small but lively temporary exhibition programme is maintained, drawing on historical and political themes, as well as reflecting the multi-cultural nature of the Borough.

The Grange Museum also houses the local history library and Borough archives, which allow historians to research in depth the history of the community in Brent. They contain a wide range of technical, literary, and historical material, and a very large collection of illustrations, as well as 19th century censuses and electoral registers.

reminder of the sometimes uneasy alliance between the past and the present, and the role of the museum in interpreting the history of its local community.

The Grange was opened in 1977 as a local history museum. It occupies a building that was erected around 1700 to form outbuildings attached to a local farm. At the beginning of the 19th century, it was converted into a cottage in the Gothic style, and was extended over the years. The building remained in use as a private residence until its purchase by the Borough Council. The museum gathers together a number of collections to illustrate life in the local community. Brent is an area that was once made up of small villages, though with the arrival of the railways and the growth of London's population, a massive increase in suburban housing transformed the landscape, particularly in the northern part of the borough. The collections reflect these rapid and sometimes radical changes. The Willesden Library collection comprises books, maps and plans, newspapers, and other two-dimensional material of importance. The Wembley History Society collection makes a substantial contribution to material from the north of the borough, and is deposited on loan to the museum. These collections are distinguished by good local photo-

graphs. Souvenirs of the British Empire Exhibition, held in 1924–25, form an attractive display.

Recent collecting at the Grange Museum has concentrated on local domestic items, to tell a more complete historical narrative. There are tools, packaging materials, clothing, and a number of objects (mainly pottery and

Demonstrators outside the Grunwick works, Willesden, 1977 (detail of painting by Dan Jones)

The Guards Museum

Wellington Barracks, Birdcage Walk,
London SW1E 6HQ
01-930 4466 ext. 3271
⊖ St James's Park
Closed Fridays. 🈺 ♿ X G
🏛 & 👥 book in advance;
special admission rates.

London is very well served by museums of military history. There are great national collections – the **Imperial War Museum, National Army Museum**, and the **Royal Armouries**; some smaller specialist museums, such as the collections of the *Royal Military School of Music* and the *Museum of Artillery in the Rotunda*; and a host of regimental collections. The newest military museum in London is a fine addition to the ranks. The Guards Museum at Wellington Barracks in Birdcage Walk has the benefit of a lovely location overlooking St James's Park, and an elegant, if rather subterranean building. The museum itself has been designed to high standards, and is notable for the quality of its presentations.

The Guards Museum tells the chronological story of the history and traditions of the five regiments of Foot Guards – the Grenadier, Scots, Welsh, Irish and Coldstream Guards – from 1650 to the present day. The display concentrates on the fighting history of the Guards, as well as their well-known ceremonial duties, such as the Trooping of the Colour.

The first experience that the visitor

A group of marching soldiers, World War II

has is of inspecting a guard of honour, walking along a line of very tall costume models wearing modern Guards uniform; most visitors will have to look up to the commanding figure of the Lieutenant Colonel of the Grenadier Guards in some awe. This display is brightly lit, and shows the uniforms in parade condition. Yet this is ultimately a museum about war and death, and later, the striking tableau of the 'Colours at the Alma', for example, shows battle-worn soldiers, one charging with a rifle fixed with a particularly vicious bayonet.

The displays begin with the English Civil War, and combine tableaux with some outstanding and important objects, such as the Dunbar Medal, and a good selection of paintings. The use of bold graphics is effective, as is the backdrop of large illustrations and photographs, which emphasise the human aspect of warfare. There are constant references to soldiers of high rank throughout the museum, but the sense of military history being shaped by countless (and nameless) soldiers of lower ranks is clearly indicated by the choice of photographs of soldiers in action. There are displays of medals and other fine memorabilia, alongside well-constructed models, and some historical oddities – the remains of a Lewis machine-gun destroyed in the Second World War with the Long Range Desert Group, or a fascinating escape kit (also from World War II) issued to the 6th Battalion Grenadier Guards, complete with map, compass, and hacksaw blade. The bloodstained surgeon's kit from the Crimean campaign is a chilling reminder of the crude medical conditions of a combat existence in the 19th century. It makes

Surgeon's kit from the Crimean campaign

Rex Whistler, The Master Cook, *1941*

an ironic contrast to the display close by in the museum of some glittering uniforms.

The chronological approach to the display covers the major high spots in the illustrious military history of the Guards – the Battle of Blenheim, the Seven Years War, the Napoleonic Wars, the Peninsular War, and the Battle of Waterloo. The history of both World Wars is covered, as is the role of the Guards in the Falklands War, with a particularly graphic reminder of the destruction of 'Sir Galahad' (and the tragic and terrible deaths of the Welsh Guards), and the night fighting on Tumbledown Mountain at the end of the campaign. These moments in recent military history are displayed without reference to the greater issues of Britain's involvement in the Falklands War, and as with other displays, record the role of the five regiments with historical accuracy, without trying to get involved with the political background.

The Guards Museum is a small and well-displayed exhibition, which will prove popular with students of military history as well as members of the general public. It is also an interesting place to view the viewers, as a large proportion of the visitors are retired members of the regiments. They read the captions and look at the displays with military precision, and attention to the minutest detail.

Gunnersbury Park Museum

Gunnersbury Park, London W3 8LQ
01-992 1612
✪ Acton Town
Open daily. 🄵 🄿
♿ **X G**: ramps to all parts of building.
🚻 & 🚻 must book in advance if tours or lectures required.

Gunnersbury Park today is the venue for a host of sporting and recreational facilities. Families come to watch and play all manner of ball games (from miniature golf to tennis and football), or to make use of the boating pond. Those who come simply to take a pleasant stroll around the park often make their way into the museum, home to one of the best collections of local history material in west London. The Gunnersbury Park Museum takes a proud place amongst the great series of 'homes in parks', which is a particularly noticeable aspect of London's museum world.

Gunnersbury Park Museum is different, though from the very grand domestic interiors retained by some of the great west London historical houses. The museum tells the story of the house as a private residence, but its message goes further than this, by reaching into the stories of ordinary and everyday life in that part of London now administered by the boroughs of Ealing and Hounslow. In doing so, and in elaborating those stories with a rich and surprising collection of objects, it becomes an extraordinary and important statement of local history.

Gunnersbury itself has had an illustrious past. The name derives from the Danish word 'Gounyldebury', which became 'Gunnalsbury' or 'Gunnals Manor'. The owner of the Manor is not known, though a legend relates that Gunhilda, the niece of King Canute, had a manor house here. Records of the appearance of the houses that appeared on the estate are scarce, though archives record some of the owners of property, such as Sir John Maynard, who commissioned the architect John Webb to build Gunnersbury House in the Palladian style (in fact modelled on Palladio's Villa Badoer near Venice) in 1663. This house was eventually demolished, and Alexander Copland, a well-known builder, purchased one of the lots on the estate created after the demolition of Gunnersbury House, building the 'Large Mansion' that now houses the museum.

The present house was altered after 1835 by the new owner, Nathan Mayer Rothschild (from the family of merchant bankers,) who wanted the estate as a country residence. Rich details like

Exterior view of Gunnersbury Park Museum

scagliola columns (made to resemble marble), and a painting of the Four Seasons on the ceiling of the Long Gallery, derive from this period of the house's history, and now form a backdrop to the museum's collection. The Rothschild story is integral to the museum, though sadly Nathan died before living at the house. His wife and son inherited the property, and it became well-known as a venue for their generous hospitality and philanthropy. The house and grounds were brought into public ownership in 1925, with a stipulation from the Rothschild trustees that the Park should be used only for leisure purposes; in 1926 Neville Chamberlain MP declared it open to the public.

The fine decorative rooms, which display the permanent museum collection, are notable for their elaborate beauty, and also for their good views of the Park, particularly looking south from the Long Gallery or the original Drawing Room.

It is the collection that first strikes the visitor on entering the museum. Well-researched narrative panels in the entrance hall describe the history of house and estate, with informative local photographs. A large printing press is on display here, important because it is documented as the earliest surviving iron press, used by the local Chiswick Press in the first half of the 19th century, and still kept in working order.

The relationship of the collection to

Rothschild Town chariot, 1820

A machinist at a Southall jeans factory: an Ed Barber photo for the 'Stitch in Time' project

working history was further emphasised on my visit in a display of costume relating to occupations, also on show in the entrance hall. A nun's habit and Women's Land Army uniform are rare survivors of working clothes from a collection rich in costume and fashion accessories. Also displayed is a single case showing a costume model wearing a man's evening suit: a coin in the donation box makes the man's top hat rise in grateful thanks – a friendly touch typical of the approachable mood of the museum.

Further inside, the visitor reaches a small temporary exhibition gallery, which has acquired a high reputation for some important community-led exhibitions. A particularly notable recent show, 'A Stitch in Time' (1987) revealed the close links between the museum and its local population by displaying the historic collection of costumes alongside a major documentary photography project, showing the work of the contemporary west London clothing trade. Photographs by Ed Barber were a colourful testament to local industries and shops, like a punjabi suit-and-children's-party-dress-makers in Southall, or a department store in Hounslow.

The theme of people making history in small but significant ways is made through many of the items on display

elsewhere – from the ever-popular group of costume accessories (anything from fans to hatpins), to toys and games. The archaeological material is very rich and displayed in a rather didactic manner. More approachable is the laundry collection (irons, domestic washing machines, and related objects), much of which came from Acton in west London, commonly known as 'Soapsud Island' due to the huge number of hand-laundries operating there from 1860 to 1940.

Trades and crafts, such as barge building and saddlery, are also featured in the displays, though the most visually compelling feature of the museum is a notable transport collection displayed in the Rothschild's Drawing Room. Contemporary photographs show a richly decorated domestic interior, complete with oriental ceramics, fine glass chandeliers, and portraits. Today, the room houses the Rothschild's 19th century town and travelling carriages and chariots, along with a hansom cab and pony phaeton. They make a bizarre – if beautifully restored – addition to the museum.

The museum is currently undertaking an extensive and long-term programme of restoration in the Victorian kitchens at the house, which are open to the public during some summer weekends.

Hackney Museum

Central Hall, Mare Street, London
E8 1HE   01-986 6914
⇌ Hackney Central
Closed Sundays and Mondays. **F**
& W G
⋔ worksheets provided for schools

Hackney Museum is one of London's newcomers. It is, by turns, a friendly, provocative, cavernous, and entertaining museum, housed in Hackney's Central Hall in a former Methodist Sunday School.

It is not long before the visitor to the museum realises that this exhibition is somehow different to many traditional displays. The clue may come first from the giant and colourful figure of Sita, a character from the Hindu epic Ramayana, made with the enthusiastic and skilful help of Purple Class at Lauriston School in the borough. Sita makes a brave statement about the full involvement of the local community in the creation of the museum, and it's that very personal contact between citizen, curator, and exhibition space that guarantees the museum's success.

Even the imposing figure of the Hindu character does not overshadow the vast hall, filled with a large collection of exhibition cases, the gallery

Headley Grafton ('Woodpecker'), Mother Earth

Builders outside new houses in Clapton passage, 1890

walls adorned with posters, photographs, and signs of the times in London – such as the witty display of a local estate agent's 'For Sale' board. The museum's collection, which is growing as the building grows into the affections and regard of the community, has been interpreted through bold and well-chosen themes. The displays may be made up of obvious and commonplace material – a Harrods radiogram, programmes for local events, an incubator – but they illustrate the history of life in a borough proud of its multi-racial mix of people, steadfast in the face of often appalling poverty and hardship, and lack of opportunities. The museum puts pictures and stories to these themes, using an impressive collection of photographs and memorabilia. Cases dealing with personal and social issues such as 'Crime and Policing', 'War against Civilians' (concerned with the Second World War in Hackney), and housing and healthcare.

These well-chosen themes can be amplified by bold choices of material. I found the election poster for Diane Abbott, MP for Hackney North and Stoke Newington (from 1987), beside text on 'the right to vote', a fitting and useful image because it enforced the sense of the life of this borough in an impressive and realistic way. The texts describing the various themes are always impartial and accurate, yet address contemporary issues in a brave and thoughtful historical context. Hackney's first municipal museum is a triumph of the ordinary made special. There is no assumption here about art for art's sake, though the museum has displayed traditional 'museum' material in its lively programme of temporary exhibitions – including mayoral silver, or works from the Chalmers Bequest of paintings. These temporary shows often reflect the particular desires of local residents (and are especially popular with them), and have included topics such as Islamic posters from Pakistan, and the Holocaust (an exhibition by a local resident concerned with the anti-fascist struggle through and after the Second World War).

At Hackney Museum's first Birthday Party in July 1988, there was considerable pride in its achievements. Diane Abbott MP referred in her speech to the rich social and political tradition of the borough, and of the need for the museum to continue to press forward with its sense and use of history.

The mixed collection at the museum has served to attract important new objects that might otherwise have been lost to public ownership. It will be interesting to see, in future years, the display of a unique 950 AD log boat, now undergoing a process of full conservation, described in graphic panels in the gallery. One Hackney councillor has donated his childhood collection of Matchbox cars (made at Lesney's toy factory at Hackney Wick in the 1950s and '60s), which is on display, and records the products of a company that closed down in 1982.

Keeping track of the transient past and present, and giving the collection an intelligible story, has been quickly and skilfully achieved at the new Hackney Museum. The museum set out, in its own words, 'to explore the roots of

Detail of a display on the right to vote and Diane Abbott, MP

the people of Hackney', and to become a museum of all Hackney's communities. Its diverse, approachable, and colourful collections render happy testimony to the early success of the museum, and the pleasure it clearly gives to a highly supportive local community.

Harrow Museum and Heritage Centre

Headstone Manor, Headstone Park, Pinner View, Harrow HA2 6PX
01-861 2626
⇌ Hatch End
Closed Mondays (except Bank holidays) and Tuesdays (except for special activities). 🅵 🅸 🅿 ♿ W G. 🚹 & 🚻 phone 01 863 6407. ☼

During the ten-minute walk from Headstone Lane railway station, the visitor to Harrow Museum and Heritage Centre passes through the pleasingly anonymous suburbs that seem to typify much of this corner of north–west London. Thoughts of Harrow's pre-Roman history (Queen Boadicea and her Icena tribe are known to have visited this area), or its rich period of Roman settlement (Brockley Hill was one of the most important pottery manufacturing centres in Roman Britain), are probably not uppermost in the visitor's mind, taking a pleasant stroll through the parkland surrounding the museum. Yet in the middle of this domestic scene is a very important group of historic buildings, now a scheduled ancient monument: Headstone Manor, the Tithe Barn, and the fire-damaged

Interior of the Tithe Barn, Harrow Museum and Heritage Centre

Small Barn, on land that includes a rare 14th century moat.

The first place to start a visit will be the beautifully-restored Tithe Barn, a ten-bayed timber-framed building with a tiled roof, known to have been built not later than 1514. The oak timbers used in the construction were probably growing during the Norman period. Three of the bays were originally partitioned off for use by the Lord of the Manor, and the remaining bays left for the use of the tenant farmer. The building is completed by two waggon-porches and a cart-shed at the rear (now converted into toilets and catering facilities). The Tithe Barn is used today by the enterprising and lively Harrow Museum and Heritage Centre as a venue for a wide range of activities, from classical music concerts and afternoon talks to lunchtime jazz recitals and tea dances.

The museum collection is gradually being built up, often through donations

Rear view of Headstone Manor

The Great or Tithe Barn

from local residents, and reflects the life and history of the area. Parts of the collection are displayed at one end of the vast cathedral-like interior of the Tithe Barn. Material relating to childhood and schooling in Harrow, or the boom in housebuilding between the wars (when a semi-detached brick villa could be bought freehold for £895) are typical of the themes selected for display. Temporary exhibitions are also held here, varying from subjects of purely local interest – such as Harrow during the First World War – to more general shows. There is also an exhibition of Whitefriars glass, which commemorates the final years of a 300-year-old industry that moved to Wealdstone in 1923, and closed down suddenly in 1980. It includes some vivid examples of workshop drawings: those by Pierre Fourmaintraux are particularly impressive (colour plate 21).

There is a friendly atmosphere about the tithe barn, which makes it feel more like a community centre than a typical local history museum.

Crossing over the medieval moat, the visit continues to some small rooms arranged for public display inside Headstone Manor. The Manor House has grown and been altered over the centuries, but it was originally constructed from the 1340s for the Archbishop of Canterbury, who held the manor. A section of the original aisled Hall still survives, although this section is currently shored up with huge timber braces. Parts of the restoration work in progress can be seen inside the house, together with architects' plans. The building has immense historic value, containing, for

Sales leaflet for newly-built houses, 1930s

example, the earliest-known crown post roof in Greater London.

The restoration project is a long-term task. Currently on display in small rooms inside the Manor are a sensitively-arranged 1930s room, and a kitchen complete with a collection of items relevant to the domestic work of the house.

The museum has exciting plans to develop its historic site by recreating the farmyard area, and relocating and possibly re-erecting important buildings dismantled from the surrounding region. The restoration of the third building on the site, the Small Barn, built in two sections in the 16th and 17th centuries, is also a priority. The museum will tell the story of Harrow through period room-settings (in the Manor), and exhibitions from the local history collection (in the Tithe Barn): its progress will be well worth watching.

The museum visitor to Harrow should also see the collection on display at the Old Speech Room Gallery in *Harrow School*. Harrow School has a long and illustrious history as a free grammar school, founded by Queen Elizabeth I in 1572 by Royal Charter. The museum displays, in an elegant and graceful modern gallery, important British watercolours, and paintings and antiquities.

Heritage Motor Museum

(British Motor Industry Heritage Trust)
Syon Park, Brentford, Middlesex TW8 8JF   01-560 1378
⊖ Gunnersbury ⇌ Syon Lane
Open daily. 🅟 Ⓖ X G
🏛 & ⛹ phone in advance; special admission rates.

Billed as 'the world's largest collection of historic British cars', the Heritage Motor Museum (run by the British Motor Industry Heritage Trust) can also lay claim to a site of great richness and historic interest – Syon Park. The museum is located in fifty-five acres of elegant parkland, with a range of other attractions, starting with *Syon House* itself (the seat of the Dukes of Northumberland), which has some astounding rooms designed by Robert Adam in 1761.

Gardening is central to the other main attractions within these quiet and gracious parklands, and a visit to Syon Park should take in, if possible, the Great Conservatory (with its Aviary and Aquarium), the Rose Garden, and the Butterfly House. This emphasis on nature makes a visit to a major collection of historic vehicles seem a surprising diversion. Certainly, the road leading to the museum feels a little like a country lane, though the stark industrial unit that houses the collection soon dispels the tranquil rural atmosphere.

Once inside the museum, the gentle light filtering through leaves and trees is replaced by the vivid, hard spotlight reflecting off around a hundred gleaming and highly-polished car bonnets. The crowded interior has the proud feel of a car showroom (without, naturally enough, the attention of enthusiastic car sales personnel), and on my visit the enthusiasm of very knowledgeable visitors added to the atmosphere of the museum.

1913 Morris Oxford Bullnose

An illustration in the original advertising brochure for the Austin 30

For those visitors whose awareness of the detailed workings of the internal combustion engine is sparse, there are helpful, if lengthy, didactic labels on technical subjects such as Power and Fuels. Each vehicle has its own information label, with basic engineering, production, and key historical information, which is more easily read. The walls around the museum are used to show supporting material in the story of British motor transport, such as sales signs, petrol pump models, and engines.

There are effective set pieces to give more of a historical context to the museum, and I found this a helpful aid in reminding me that motor transport is a substantial feature of 20th century life. The reconstruction of the John Carter and Son Garage at Pentlepoir (though suspiciously, if inevitably, too clean) gives an inkling of motoring in a more relaxed age (colour plate 2), and compares well with a set piece of a 1970s road rally.

The museum, in the main, lets the cars speak for themselves, each vehicle making its own style statement about an opulent age of grand touring, or the modern habit of convenience driving. There are curiosities, failures, and great industrial success stories woven into this metal narrative, and a visit to the museum is primarily enjoyable for putting the cars into a social and historical context. Probably everyone has a view on the ill-fated Sinclair C5, for example, which stands rather forlornly alongside more familiar and traditional vehicles. Clive Sinclair's electric three-wheeled vehicle made a major media impact in 1985, but simply did not sell. Yet it probably made more people think about the need for alternative methods of transport than any other recent vehicle, and as such has an important place in the history of vehicle development, and a rightful place in this important museum.

In some ways the Sinclair C5 – for all the technological sophistication of its production – reminded me of great cars such as the Morris Oxford Bullnose from the early years of this century. The museum has a fine 1913 example, which probably gave just an uncomfortable a ride, though the dignified wooded steering wheel and the gleaming radiator must have added class to any journey.

This museum in fact hints at themes like the car as a class symbol, the changing patterns of driving and expectations of passenger comfort, and the devotion of most research energies to technological advances. But if you look carefully around the galleries, and particularly at the impressive full-colour catalogue, the social themes that enrich the story of motor transport become clearer. There are, for example, stories of product marketing and consumer hopes in every page of the museum's collection of advertising posters and leaflets (many illustrated in the catalogue), which relay signals of the 'motoring as joy' message also transmitted by the museum. I would recommend glancing through the catalogue before a visit; the historical context of the British Motor Industry is clearly described, and the more de-

1971 Morris 1800S MkII

Sinclair C5

pressing tale of the industrial effects caused by the serious decline in Britain's capacity as a volume car producer hinted at.

The museum will appeal to anyone with an interest in the history of the car, and the arrangement of vehicles, which allows visitors to walk around most cars, is thoughtful. The collection includes some rather precarious 19th century tricycles and bicycles, as well as costumes. But chiefly, it presents a comprehensive and gleamingly-restored survey of cars from an 1895 Wolseley Tricar and 1897 Daimler, through grand and stately Rover and Standards from the early years of this century, to cars such as the Morris Eight, Standard Vanguard and MG Midget, which, along with many other cars in this impressive collection, will have an abiding place in the history of the British Motor Industry. Cars on display are changed from time to time: the British Motor Industry Heritage Trust has preserved over 300 vehicles, all in working order (and often loaned out for use in films, television, and so on); the Trust also operates the British Commercial Vehicle Museum at Leyland, near Preston (described in the North–West England *Exploring Museums* guide).

The Heritage Motor Museum at Syon Park is a good place to make a nostalgic visit to see popular cars in showroom condition, and to reflect on the possibilities of driving styles into the next century.

The Horniman Museum and Library

100 London Road, Forest Hill, London SE23 3PQ
01-699 2339/ 1872/4911
⇄ Forest Hill (some distance)
Closed Sunday mornings. **F** ▣
♿ **T X G**: no wheelchair access to top floors.
♀♂ must book in advance: contact Senior Teacher at Education Centre. ◉

'This building and its contents being a portion of a gift from Frederick John Horniman MP to the London County Council as representing the people of London, are dedicated to the public for ever as a free museum for their recreation, instruction and enjoyment.' So reads the memorial plaque outside one of London's great museums, 'The Horniman'.

Today, around a quarter of a million visitors a year make the journey to Forest Hill. Visits remain forever in affections and loyal memories, particularly those of London parents and children, for the Horniman is perhaps London's best-loved museum. This feeling of affection is due to the great abundance of the museum's varied collections, the highly-regarded and immensely popular education programmes, and the vision and philanthropy of Horniman himself.

Frederick Horniman, MP for Falmouth and member of the famous family tea-firm, was an energetic, kindly man, who had been obsessed since childhood by the idea of collecting – at the outset mainly butterflies, moths and insects, and other natural history material. His passion for collecting increased as he began to travel throughout the world on the firm's business, to the point where his home at Forest Hill, called 'Surrey House', could no longer hold his collection. Eventually, Horniman and his family moved to the adjoining 'Surrey Mount', and opened the 'Surrey House Museum' regularly to the public from 1890. It was an immediate success, not least due to the fine surroundings of the Horniman Gardens. The current museum is a purpose-built gallery opened in 1901, designed for Horniman by C. Harrison Townsend in the Art Nouveau style,

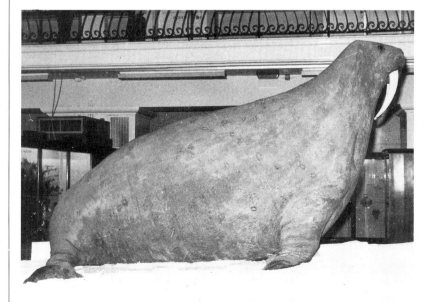

The Horniman Museum Walrus

Robert Anning Bell's mosaic panel on the front of the building

and distinguished by its tall clock tower, and a fine mosaic panel at the front of the building, symbolising the moral, intellectual, and spiritual meaning of life.

The mosaic's theme is a grand one for the start of any museum visit, but there is nothing off-putting inside. The Horniman has a friendly, crowded, intriguing feel about it. It is a museum that grows on you, with a slightly old-fashioned atmosphere about its grand exhibition cases and towering galleries. It feels just like a real museum ought to feel, packed with fascinating, diverse, and entertaining things: a 'museum of world heritage' that really does live up to its name.

The collections at the Horniman Museum are divided into three distinct yet related groups. The Ethnography material looks at customs and beliefs, arts and crafts. The Musical Instrument collection is one of the most important in Britain, and is truly international in its range. Finally, the museum has an outstanding Natural History collection, reflecting Horniman's own early interests, and containing everything from mammals, birds, fish, reptiles, and fossils to a very popular aquarium. Each gallery has been carefully laid out in sections, with, for example, the rich mask collection shown as a group, an area devoted to religious beliefs (Hinduism, Buddhism, and so on) and the musical instruments sub-divided into types; like stringed instruments or drums.

Headdress commissioned from Mbuke artist Patrick Adeh Achong of Odaje, Ogoza, early 1970s

Everybody will have their own favourite object, whether it's the perky spotted seahorse in the aquarium, an object like the face mask by John Martin (b.1941), made from material found beachcombing along the Thames, which was on loan at the time of my visit, or some wonderfully intricate and colourful musical instruments, like the pair of Western African Kora displayed side by side (an original 19th century example next to one made by Aliu Suso in 1985). But no one could miss the Great Walrus – something of a symbol, now, for this museum. The walrus from Hudson Bay belongs to the museum's earliest days, and was one of the original creatures on display to the public. Mounted in 1870, it rises with extraordinary bulk from an artificial ice-flow, a dignified and massive reminder of the museum's longevity.

Making faces – an education project on masks

Don't miss the chance to compare your weight with that of the walrus by standing on the nearby scales. Those with more of an interest in works of art will not be disappointed by the sheer scale and virtuosity of the Apostle clock on the top floor of the museum. It is a German clock (currently under restoration), made in 1860, and shows scenes from Christ's life. When the clock is in motion, the apostles move past Christ, bowing their heads – save Judas, who turns his back.

The Horniman Museum is big enough to make a number of repeat visits worthwhile: there always seems to be something new and fascinating to see. Yet the museum activities only begin with looking at things in the galleries. The Horniman runs a staggering range of courses and classes, from fish-keeping to pottery workshops, dance and music, as well as the ever-popular boomerang competitions. There are free lectures and concerts, and major exhibitions, and the Horniman Gardens can be explored, with their variety of nature trails, and sunken and water gardens.

The museum has recently produced a very attractive, colourful, and informative guide to the collections. It has a helpful plan, and suggests nine different things to see for the visitor with only an hour to spare. The guide also contains a fetching, full-size cutout mask.

Imperial War Museum
Lambeth Road, London SE1 6HZ
01-735 8922
⊖ Lambeth North ⇌ Waterloo
Open daily. ▣▣ ♿ X G
♿ & ♿ book in advance through
Education Department.

The approach to the Imperial War Museum leaves the visitor in no doubt as to its forbidding subject. As you pass through an attractive and colourful rose garden there is no escape from the sight of the huge twin barrels of a Royal Navy 15 inch gun. It is, as the information label coyly puts it, 'one of the most accurate and reliable weapons ever produced for the Royal Navy'. There is nothing deadpan about the interpretation of war inside this impressive museum, however: nowhere does it shirk the reality of wholesale destruction or death, or glory in war for its own sake. Instead there is a forceful, historically-accurate narrative, which puts war into its political, social, and economic context, with constant emphasis on the outcome of war as a result of human decisions with human consequences.

The museum building itself was formerly the central section of Bethlem Royal Hospital, or Bedlam, completed in 1815, with the spectacular and instantly-recognisable copper dome added in 1846. Bethlem Royal Hospital, which began to specialise in the care of the insane during the 14th century, has occupied many buildings in London. It was transferred from this site in Southwark to Eden Park in Bromley in 1930. The Imperial War Museum was founded by the Government in 1917, specifically as a National War Museum to display material relating to the Great War, as it was being fought. It, too, has had varied sites, from Crystal Palace to the Imperial Institute, and was opened to the public here in 1936.

The new galleries that are scheduled to open to the public in 1989 will revolutionise the appearance of the building. Behind the neo-classical

Soldier writing home from the front, First World War

Dame Laura Knight, Ruby Loftus screwing a breechring, *1943*

Paul Nash, Wire, *1918*

brick entrance-façade a huge steel barrel-vaulted shed will contain new galleries, and the courtyards will be restored to made a dramatic backdrop to the new building. Every attempt will be made in the new galleries, on four floors of exhibition space, to bring the story of war in the 20th century alive by the use of interactive exhibits, and state-of-the-art display techniques.

The role of the Imperial War Museum is to display and preserve material that describes the two world wars, and all other conflicts and military operations that have involved Britain and the Commonwealth countries since 1914. This is a huge and unique museum undertaking, and the collections used to support the never-ending story of war are of great scope and size. The First World War collections are typically diverse. They include all manner of material, from archive photographs of the terrible conflict in the trenches to patriotic recruiting posters. The museum has the guns that fired the first British shells of the war at sea and land, along with the grim weapons of war used in trench fighting, from knives and knuckledusters to a crossbow adapted for use as a grenade-launcher, found in German trenches in 1915.

The development of the tank broke the deadlock in trench warfare, and the museum has an example of the early manoeuvrable Mark V model, as well as British aircraft, which grew to have an influential tactical role at the end of the conflict. The salvaged engine from the wreckage of the Fokker Dr I triplane flown by Baron von Richthofen – the most renowed fighter pilot in the

View of entrance to Imperial War Museum

war – is one of the many unique objects in the collection.

One of the most moving ways of expressing life during wartime is through the work of the artist. The Imperial War Museum holds a major collection of paintings, drawings, prints, and sculptures, which includes works commissioned from official war artists, and poster designs by anonymous artists which often emphasised the threatened tranquil rural joys of Britain. There are particularly fine works by Paul Nash, Stanley Spencer, and Laura Knight.

One of the most authentic ways of transmitting the reality of warfare is through sound recordings. The museum holds the national archive in its Department of Sound Records, including oral history interviews (like, for example, projects with combat cameramen in the Second World War, and with war artists from the Falklands campaign), broadcast recordings and sound documents, such as lectures on defence policy, and sound effects associated with war. The Film Department maintains an enormous archive, from record film of military operations to propaganda films and war newsreels.

Collections relating to the Second World War are also impressive, and stress the conditions of warfare as well as political and military aspects. The use of video, reconstructions, and models, along with sound effects, make a compelling story, and there are important and once all-too-familiar objects, such as the Anderson shelter used during air raids, as well as unique material like the caravans used by Field-Marshal Montgomery as his tactical headquarters in the field. The museum has also built up collections relating to conflicts since 1945, and these are displayed to consider the implications of chemical and nuclear warfare.

There are two 'outstations' of the Imperial War Museum in London that are also worth visiting. HMS 'Belfast' is permanently moored on the river Thames as a museum that illustrates the story of life on board a Royal Navy cruiser. The 'Belfast' saw action in the Second World War and during the Korean War. The *Cabinet War Rooms*, by St James's Park, show the underground emergency accommodation that was created to give Winston Churchill, the War Cabinet, and the Chiefs of Staff protection during air attacks in the Second World War. It is a large complex of twenty-one rooms, including the Prime Minister's Room and the Cabinet Room.

The Iveagh Bequest, Kenwood

Hamstead Lane, London NW3 7JR
01-348 1286/7
⊖Archway, Golders Green (some distance)
Closes 4pm from 1 Oct. to Maundy Thursday. F ☕ P
♿ W ground floor, S upper, G, but most exhibits downstairs.
🚻 & 👥 by arrangement with Curator.
Open air concerts on Saturday evenings in July and August (01 734 1877 for details).

Walking through the lovely grounds that surround Kenwood, or listening to one of the summer lakeside concerts held there, are unforgettable experiences in themselves; combine this with a visit to the Iveagh Bequest, Kenwood, and you have one of the great artistic visits in London.

Kenwood has come through something of a turbulent history. The house itself was saved from demolition by the

Sir Anthony Van Dyck, Henrietta of Lorraine, *1634*

Jan Vermeer, The Guitar Player, *before 1676*

Earl of Iveagh in 1925, and he bequeathed to the people of London the extraordinary collection of paintings that is on display today. It was Lord Iveagh's wish to preserve the house, together with its contents, 'as a fine example of the artistic house of a gentleman of the 18th century'. His collection of paintings (purchased in the 1880s and 1890s) would have stood comparison with any American private collection; the new furnishings were less judiciously chosen, and when the house opened to the public in 1928 it presented an appearance of domesticity that it had never really enjoyed. Lord Iveagh in fact only spent a few nights at Kenwood, and the show of a 'gentleman's' house was an artificial one.

Slowly but surely the nature of Kenwood House was changed, in a careful and triumphant attempt to give it a genuine 18th century character. Fine examples of 18th century cabinet making were skilfully added to the House, and Adam furniture, similar to pieces lost when the original furnishings were sold in 1922, was bought to complement the displays.

Kenwood itself is an imposing and attractive Geogian mansion, which was remodelled in the fashionable neoclassical style for Lord Mansfield, the famous Lord Chief Justice. Lord Mansfield commissioned this work

from the foremost architect and designer, Robert Adam, between 1764–73.
Adam designed much of the interior
decoration and furnishing, with the
great Library proving the outstanding
room in the house (colour plate 14).
The pale colour, harmonious symmetry, classical use of pillars, and the very
precise detailing of gliding and plasterwork all stand as a reminder of the
work of a great designer at the outset of
his creative powers.

The collection of paintings at Kenwood would have to be superlative not
to be overshadowed by this stunning
room – and it is. Evenly dispersed
throughout the galleries, the collection
is modest enough in size to be seen
without making the visitor tired, and
there are famous and beautiful pictures
in every room. The collection is strong
in paintings of the English, Dutch and
French schools. Perhaps the best-
known work is Rembrandt's 'Self-
Portrait', in the Dining Room, a painting that has a dark but not sombre
colour, and a hauntingly brave, wistful,
and even grave sense of character. In
the Parlour there is an especially striking portrait, recently added to the collection, by the Italian painter Pompeo
Batoni (1708–87). It shows Mrs
Isabella Sandilands, clearly a vigorous,
healthy, and bright personality. This is

Rembrandt van Rijn, Self-portrait, c. *1663*

Thomas Gainsborough, Two Shepherd Boys
with Dogs Fighting, *exhibited 1783*

a fresh and beautiful portrait well
worth studying.

The dazzlingly light Orangery at
Kenwood currently shows two of Thomas Gainsborough's late 'fancy' paintings. They are massive yet freely
painted. The 'Shepherd Boys With
Dogs Fighting' (1787) has elements of
playfulness and real violence, whereas
the sketchy quality of the painting of
'Greyhounds coursing a Fox' catches
the fox's death-struggle painfully and
accurately. It is an important work,
since it is the only example of a sporting scene by Gainsborough without
human figures.

The Music Room contains some
elegant portraits by Reynolds and
Romney, along with some fine musical
instruments. A graceful early-19th-
century Grecian Harp stands in front
of the large mahogany chamber organ
(made by John England and Son
around 1780), which would have
formed an integral part of any late-
18th-century Music Room. There are
some fine examples of grand 18th century furniture throughout the House,
as well as some unusual pieces. The
Mechanical Invalid, or 'Gouty' chair by
John Joseph Merlin (1735–1803) looks
what it is – a particularly comfortable
prototype wheelchair. The 'Titus'
clock is an elegant example, made by
Matthew Boulton for George III in
1772, with a vivid representation of the
Roman Emperor in a toga, beside the
inscription *Diem Perdidi.*

The Jewish Museum

Woburn House, Tavistock Square, London WC1H OEP 01-388 4525
⊖ Euston, Euston Square, Russell Square ⇌ Euston
Closed Friday afternoons Sept–March, Jewish and Public holidays, Saturdays and Mondays. **V**
& **XG**, lift.
♿ & **♿** phone in advance, **♿** **F**; talks and guided tours by arrangement.

A memorable collection, though one that is a little difficult to track down, is found in the single room now housing the Jewish Museum on an upper floor of Woburn House in the centre of London.

The establishment of the museum goes back to 1932, when Woburn House was opened as a communal centre, with a small museum of Jewish ceremonial art and antiquities. The latter was created from private loans, gifts and purchases, including superb ritual silver from the Franklin Collection, books and manuscripts from Jews' College, decorative art from early City of London synagogues, and a good collection of paintings. There are some particularly important items of Jewish ritual art purchased from the Arthur Howitt Collection, including a three-tiered spice box made in Germany around 1700, with unusual decoration of enamelled pictures.

The museum's collection has grown steadily to this day, and is displayed in cramped surroundings to illustrate themes of Jewish life and religion, with particular relevance to the lives of the Jewish community in Britain. It is a choice, and in some cases spectacular gathering of objects – from Torah scrolls to ark curtains, marriage mugs and illuminated marriage contracts to loving cups. It is one of the most crowded small museums in London, but somehow the dense arrangement of precious objects makes the visitor look even more closely at individual pieces. It is certainly worth taking time, for example, to study some of the intricate detail in the imposing collec-

Silver Chanuka lamp

tion of silver and brass Hanukah lamps.

One object casts a dramatic and unmistakable presence over the whole museum, however – the rich and elaborately carved synagogue ark, which is of Italian 16th century work. It was used to house the Scrolls of the Law, handwritten on parchment by a special scribe. This particular example was discovered at a sale at Chillingham Castle in Northumberland, where it had a rather unceremonious history, being used as a wardrobe in one of the servant's bedrooms. It has been carefully restored, and is one of the finest objects in the museum.

Also worth seeing is the 'Vanitas' painting by Benjamin Senior Godines (colour plate 20), painted in Amsterdam in 1681. Dutch Vanitas paintings were intended to point out the transitory nature of life, with Hebrew and Spanish inscriptions enforcing the message of inevitable death and bodily corruption. On a more cheering note, the museum displays fine examples of its distinguished collection of Anglo-Jewish silver, with three important 18th century presentation pieces given to the Lord Mayor of London. The salver

Faience pottery Passover Dish

and two cups reflect a Dutch custom of presenting an annual gift of plate together with chocolates or sweetmeats, which the Spanish and Portuguese congregation of the city gave to the Lord Mayor. The tiny Byzantine gold votive plaque with embossed Jewish symbols is one of the very rare survivals of Jewish antiquity, dating from the 7th or 8th century. It was probably used to ornament the Torah, or Scrolls of the Law.

One aspect of the collection offers a surprising but entertaining departure from grand and formal religious art – the story of sport. On a Staffordshire

Silver-gilt Torah finials by Samuel Edlin, London 1712

John Wesley's House and the Museum of Methodism

49 City Road, London EC1Y 1AU
01-253 2262
⊖Moorgate, Old Street (exit 4)
⇌ Moorgate
Open daily. 🅂
♿ **SG**: steps to crypt where Museum of Methodism is housed.
🏛 & 🚻 phone The Secretary at least 14 days in advance.

John Wesley (1703–91), the founder of the Methodist Church, lived in this simple and unassuming Georgian House from 1779 until his death. With a friend and with his brother, Charles, Wesley established a religious group whilst at college in Oxford, which earned them the name 'Methodist', due to their regular and methodical pattern of study and worship. Wesley's House, the adjacent Wesley's Chapel, and the Museum of Methodism are all testament to his devoted and energetic life spent proclaiming his religious faith, both all over Britain and in America.

Wesley's House is now a suitably plain and old-fashioned museum staffed by welcoming volunteers. The house has been well restored, is obviously cherished, and has a quiet and rather monochrome atmosphere relieved only by the splash of colour provided by a modern (1947) stained glass mural on the staircase, showing Wesley preaching to a crowd. The collection that is used to illustrate the story of Wesley's life and evangelical work varies from mementoes to objects owned by the greatest methodist preacher (such as Wesley's fork). There are some quaint pieces, like the section of tree-trunk 'under which Wesley preached at his last open-air service on October 7th 1790 aged 87 years' and, tucked away in various cabinets, a very important collection of 19th century commemorative ceramics with Wesleyan motifs.

There are interesting historic items in abundance in the Study of the house – in particular Wesley's own walnut bureau, his travelling robe and three-cornered hat, and the chair Wesley used to preside over the first Methodist

mug and jug, dating from the early 19th century, are printed scenes of the famous boxing match between Daniel Mendoza and Richard Humphreys in 1788. Mendoza had an influential part to play in the development of boxing, and his career was historically important in that his exploits in the boxing ring encouraged a more favourable attitude amongst the British public towards Jews. The small ceramic collection in the museum is enhanced by some colourful 18th and 19th century figures of Jewish pedlars, describing an aspect of British social history, as in a different way does the English mid-19th-century papier mâché table with a fine painting of the interior of the New Synagogue in London.

Scholars of Jewish art and antiquities will refer to the important catalogues of the museum; the ordinary visitor should keep a watch out for the series of small temporary exhibitions. It is worth seeing the two audio-visual presentations that describe Jewish festivals and ceremonies, which put the mixed collection of objects into context. The illustrated guidebook also provides helpful summaries of Jewish customs.

18th century caricature of John Wesley and Methodism

Conference in 1744. Wesley's library is shown in a stately mahogany bookcase.

Perhaps the most powerful and evocative room in the house is the Prayer Room, which has been simply arranged with the preacher's chair, table, kneeler, candlestick, and snuffer. Wesley is known to have begun each day in London here, at four in the morning, writing of the experience: 'Here then I am far from the busy ways of man'. On the top floor of the House, where Wesley's preachers once used to stay, is the museum room with a varied group of personal belongings and commemorative ceramics. This gallery also contains the most surprising object in the collection, the electric-shock machine that Wesley used to treat patients suffering from depression who attended his clinics.

Visitors to the House should take the opportunity of seeing Wesley's Chapel next door. He described it as 'perfectly neat, but not fine'. It is notable for the original pulpit, and the jaspar pillars that support the gallery. These were originally ships' masts and were given by George III. When built, the chapel had the largest single-span plaster ceiling in London. In the crypt there is a modern, well-laid-out museum telling the story of Methodism from its development in the 18th century to the present day. Well-illustrated narrative panels discuss themes such as 'Methodism Comes of Age' or

Robert Hunter, John Wesley, *1765*

'Methodism and the Arts', and these are interspersed with cases containing more of the important collection of Wesleyan decorative arts. Particularly attractive are the early 19th century pottery models of Wesleyan chapels. It is also possible to walk around the display to the accompaniment of a cheerful Wesleyan hymn. Displayed close to the entrance of the museum is a memorable curiosity, a portrait of John Wesley in 20,000 words of microscopic scripts by Gluck Rosenthal – the result of three years' patient writing.

On leaving the museum it is worth visiting Wesley's tomb in the graveyard behind the chapel. Ten minutes' walk away, near the main entrance of the **Museum of London**, a massive metal flame commemorates Wesley's conversion on May 24th, 1738.

Visitors who would prefer a complete contrast to this quiet and unassuming museum should cross City Road to the headquarters of the *Honourable Artillery Company*, to see their recently-opened museum, with an important and well-displayed collection of military costume and medals.

Interior view of Wesley's Chapel

Keats House

Wentworth Place, Keats Grove, Hampstead, London NW3 2RR
01-435 2062
⊖ Hampstead ⇌ Hampstead Heath
Closed every morning except Saturday. 🅵 ♿ **SG**
🍴 & 👥 arrange in advance with Assistant Curator.

Keats House is beautifully situated in a quiet Hampstead street. The entrance, along a path lined with lavender bushes, gives a restful approach to one of the gems in London's community of small, specialist museums.

Keats House was the home of the poet John Keats (1795–1821) for two years before his tragic early death. Hampstead then was very much a country village, but one that had a reputation as the centre of an artistic community (very much as it does today, in fact). Keats met his fellow poets, Shelley and John Hamilton Reynolds, at Hampstead, along with painters such as Joseph Severn and Benjamin Robert Haydon. He was already living in Hampstead when he was introduced to the owners of two semi-detached houses (Wentworth Place), which had been built in 1815–16. One was let in 1819 to a Mrs Brawne, a widow with three children. Keats was introduced,

Fanny Brawne, c. 1850

Keats's bedroom, with a bed similar to the one Keats would have occupied

Front view of Keats House

and formed an attachment to Fanny, the eldest daughter, then aged eighteen. At this time he was caring for his sick brother Tom, who was dying of consumption, and upon calling on his friend Charles Armitage Brown (who lived in one of the houses) to tell him of Tom's death, was persuaded to stay at Wentworth Place.

Keats found himself living next to Fanny Brawne in a peaceful and healthy environment, which inspired him not only to read prodigiously, but also to compose verse. Some of Keats's best-known work was written at Wentworth Place – the odes 'To the Nightingale' (written under a plum tree in the garden), 'On Melancholy', and 'La Belle Dame sans Merci', for example.

Today Keats House has an elegant, and above all carefully-kept atmosphere. The rooms have been extensively restored, and are furnished in an authentic Regency style. The house has a considerable collection of Keats memorabilia, with the objects described on very beautifully handwritten captions. Keats house is now set out with the rooms that Keats himself occupied (his sitting room and bedroom), together with Charles

Brown's sitting room. The Brawne Rooms are a touching memorial to Keats and Fanny Brawne. On their engagement, Keats gave Fanny a ring set with an almandine; she wore this until her death, and it is now displayed in the museum, with more of Fanny's property gifted to Keats House by her granddaughter. Also on display in the Brawne Room is a Hepplewhite dining table that used to belong to Leigh Hunt, the well-known critic and journalist, who had read, admired, and published Keats's early poem, 'To Solitude'.

Keats's bedroom on the upper floor is still a hauntingly sad part of the house, though there have been many structural alterations to the room since 1820. It has been displayed in a style that is appropriate to the period, and the Regency tent-bed is similar to the bed Keats would have occupied during his final illness. Keats's friend, Brown, nursed him at this time, and recalls the tragic moment when Keats coughed blood on his sheet, looked at the single drop, and 'After regarding it steadfastly, . . . looked up in my face, with a calmness of countenance that I can never forget, and said, -"I know the

colour of that blood; – it is arterial blood; – I cannot be deceived in that colour; – that drop of blood is my death warrant; – I must die".' Keats, who had been apprenticed to a local surgeon when living in Edmonton, and had studied medicine at Guy's and St Thomas's, knew what he was talking about. He died eventually of pulmonary tuberculosis, the disease that had killed his brother Tom, though he recovered sufficiently to make a painful journey from Hampstead to spend the winter in Italy, on the advice of his doctors. He died in Rome, with the elegiac epitaph, 'Here lies one whose name was writ in water', inscribed on his tomb.

Wentworth Place was bought in 1838 by the actress Eliza Chester, who converted the two houses into one, and added an elegant and spacious drawing room and conservatory, now known as the Chester Room. A portrait by John Jackson of Eliza Chester is displayed over the fireplace, and here also is a coloured print that recalls her most highly-regarded part as Lady Teazle in Sheridan's *School for Scandal*. The Chester Room displays important objects from the permanent Keats Collection, including letters, literary manuscripts, the poet's writing desk and inkstand, and the anatomical notebook from Keats's days as a medical student.

Adjacent to Keats House is a modern (1931) building, now a public library. The unique and important Keats Memorial Library is kept at Wentworth Place, and comprises over 8000 volumes relating to Keats and his contemporary poets (it is only available by appointment to researchers).

Kensington Palace
Court Dress Collection and State Apartments

Kensington Palace, London W8 4PX
01-937 9561
⊖ High Street Kensington, Queensway
Closed Sunday mornings. 🖻 ⚴ S
🏛 & 👫 book in advance giving two weeks' notice, 👫 🄵 on completion of application form.

In 1689, William III bought a fine Jacobean House from the Earl of Nottingham, and engaged Christopher Wren and Nicholas Hawksmoor to remodel the property, which had the benefit of a spacious and open country setting. Today, Kensington Palace looks out over Kensington Gardens and Hyde Park, and since 1984 has had on display the Court Dress Collection, in restored Victorian rooms on the Garden Floor. A joint ticket admits visitors to the Collection, and to the magnificent State Apartments of Kensington Palace.

Kensington Palace itself has been a royal residence ever since William III's day. William and Queen Mary, Queen Anne and George II, all died at the Palace, and Queen Victoria was born here, reputedly in the North Drawing Room. This room can be seen in the trip around the Court Dress Collection, and has been renovated according to an inventory of 1820.

The entrance to the display of costume is suitably grand, through an orientation gallery where the ritualistic world of Court, Drawing Room, and Levée are introduced to the sound of stately music. The rooms that are used to display the Collection were originally occupied by the Duke and Duchess of Kent and Princess Victoria (their daughter), who lived at the Palace until her accession to the Throne in 1837. The Red Saloon, where Queen Victoria sat before the Accession Council, is also on the tour, and in common with all of the period rooms has been meticulously restored and furnished to its Victorian appearance.

These large, lavish, and bright rooms form a welcome contrast in style and appearance to the galleries displaying costume from the Court Dress Collection. Here the lighting is kept strictly to the low levels recommended by conservators to ensure that the delicate and light-sensitive fabrics do not fade. For this reason, too, the costumes are taken off display from time to time, and new selections arranged. It will only take a few moments for one's eyes to adjust to the dim lighting levels, and the information panels have been carefully designed to make them clear and easy to read. The layout of costumes is in chronological order, dating from the mid-18th century to the 1930s. The first set of dresses and uniforms displayed concentrates on individual styles and shapes – the dress as an 'art object', to be looked at for its own sake. This approach is helpfully followed by grand room reconstructions, covering appropriate themes and periods, such as 'Court Dress 1835–70', 'Levée Dress Uniform', or 'After an Evening Court'. There is also a small temporary

Wedding dress of Lady Diana Spencer

exhibition gallery in which, over the summer months, thematic displays are organised to highlight special interest areas of the Collection.

Entering the bizarre and ritualistic world of Court Dress is a vivid reminder of the opulence (and somehow the deep irelevance) of aristocratic life, with its detailed regulations of behaviour and appearance, its arcane language, and its bewildering snobbery.

Lady's Court Dress and uniform of King's Bodyguard for Scotland, 1912

Before 1815 the main requirement for dress worn by gentlemen at Court was that is should be splendid. After that time, rules of dress were imposed, and very rigidly applied; particular uniforms thereby developed for Court appearances. Ladies dress for Court had been governed by written rule, and unwritten convention, since about 1730. 18th century Ladies Court dress took the form of a mantua (open gown) and petticoat, and is especially characterised by the wearing of extraordinarily wide hoops. Certain elements of Ladies Court dress were retained over a long period of time, notably the low-cut bodice, and long, flowing train, very grandly shown, for example, in a Lady's Court dress of about 1870, of cream silk with a bold satin stripe in purple and yellow (colour plate 11). Male dress was likewise strictly regulated, members of the services wearing full dress uniforms, and other men appearing in military-style costumes fashioned according to rules published by the Lord Chamberlain's Office. Swords were a regular part of men's Court dress.

There were many opportunities to parade these elaborate costumes. In the 18th century the Court was an important feature in political life; favour at Court might lead to royal appointments, and influence could be sought in the discreet conversations that no doubt took place. The 'Drawing Room', however, became a significant event in the social season when this occasion was taken to present young ladies to the monarch. Under Edward VII, this afternoon ceremony was superceded by the glittering Evening Courts. Gentlemen, throughout this period, were presented at Levées. The last Evening Court and Levée were held in 1939.

An article published in *Punch* in 1840, quoted in the well-written and beautifully illustrated colour guide book to the Court Dress Collection, makes some telling points about this British infatuation with formal presentations to royalty: 'The real truth is that the court dress is a masquerade costume', it states, noting that 'it is well known that [Queen Victoria holds her Levées] for the good of trade, chiefly', to promote 'British manufacturing industry'.

The sumptuous display of formal Court dress on show at Kensington Palace is well worth seeing, both as a reminder of a long-lost way of life for the few, and as a tribute to some lavish and beautifully detailed costumes.

View of the Court at St James, with a lady being presented to Her Majesty, c. 1770

Kew Bridge Steam Museum

Green Dragon Lane, Brentford, Middlesex TW8 OEN 01-568 4757
⊖ Gunnersbury ⇌ Kew Bridge
Open daily. 'In Steam' at weekends and on Bank Holiday Mondays. 🎧
▣ 🅿
♿ S: steps to old engine houses.
🚹 & 🚺 by special arrangement; steamings of on weekdays are held in May and October for schools. ◉

A short walk from Kew Bridge railway station lies one of London's unsung cultural communities. Along Kew Bridge Road, towards Brentford High Street, there are a number of important heritage sites offering a complementary range of attractions, from an international collection of musical instruments (in *The Musical Museum*) to a renowned Arts Centre (Watermans) and the pastoral delights of Syon Park, complete with its museum of historic British vehicles (the **Heritage Motor Museum**).

At the start of this museum trail is one of the most commanding buildings of all: Kew Bridge Pumping Station. This museum is in complete contrast to leafy Syon Park at the other end of the main road. The site comprises grand, towering, industrial buildings, their adjacent land dotted with a curious assortment of boats, engines, and steamrollers. The gracious brick standpipe tower of the pumping station might today be overshadowed by nearby tower blocks, but it still remains an imposing industrial image.

The museum is busily intent on a great programme of reorganisation and redisplay. The restoration project for the buildings themselves, as well as the highly important collection of engines, continues to be a major exercise. It is explained rather forlornly in one label asking for the public's understanding for the state of disarray brought about by ambitious plans for a new museum of water, and the contruction, around the grounds, of a narrow-gauge railway and new workshops.

Giant beam of 100" engine

It is easy to forget the work in progress once inside the 19th century buildings of the former Grand Junction Waterworks Company's Pumping Station. The site was chosen for its proximity to the north bank of the Thames, from which the great engines drew the water supply for London. The museum is open during the week but a visit during the weekend is particularly recommended, since the museum is then 'in steam'. At the heart of the collection are five magnificent Cornish beam pumping engines, which were active for over a hundred years until 1944. The massive Cornish engines, developed by renowned Cornish engineers such as Richard Trevithick and Jonathan Hornblower, were originally designed to pump out the water from the county's tin and copper mines. Their 19th-century designs were so efficient and advanced that few changes had to be made to engines built in the early 20th century. Three of the engines are operated under steam (along with some engines from other buildings). One of the pleasures associated with any visit – quite apart from the magnificent spectacle of the working parts of the great machines – is the self-evident pride on the faces of the museum maintenance engineers as they watch over the engines at work. The museum is a place with the drama of an industrial site. The use of working models and miscellaneous collec-

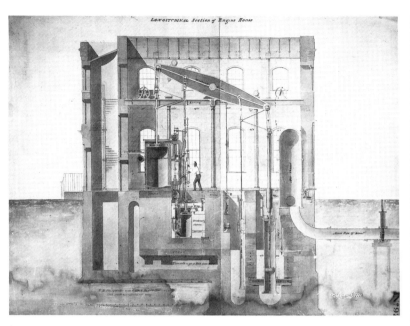

Section through an engine house with Boulton and Watt engine

Kingston Upon Thames Museum and Heritage Centre

Wheatfield Way, Kingston Upon Thames, Surrey KT1 2PS
01-546 5386
⇌ Kingston
Closed Sundays. **F**
&. **X** ground floor; upper floor inaccessible to wheelchair users; **G**.
⚥ & ⚥ pre-book only if guided tours required.

In Kingston's modern town centre, next to the Guildhall, a grey sandstone slab, the Coronation Stone, stands as a reminder of the historic importance of this part of south-west London. Traditionally, it is the stone on which seven Saxon kinds were crowned, and the Borough's strong royal connections were marked by the confirmation of Kingston upon Thames as a Royal Borough by George V in 1927.

Kingston developed as a major mar-

tions relating to the history of London's water supply add to the central spectacle of the beautifully-restored engines.

The pride and joy of this unique collection is the great pair of a 90 inch and a 100 inch Cornish beam engine – the largest waterworks engines in the world. A steep but elegant group of stairways allows the visitor today to walk beside the engines to the giant beams and crank wheels at their summit. It is a great soaring climb inside a great industrial monument. These two

A professional blacksmith at work, Kew Bridge Steam Museum

engines in harness provided most of the station's pumping capacity, and though the machines bear an elegant grandeur of design and appearance today, working them in a commercial environment must have been far less romantic.

The museum's oldest engine is an 1820 example of a Boulton and Watt 'West Cornish' engine, which was built originally for the Grand Junction Waterworks site at Chelsea. It can pump 130 gallons at each stroke.

Kew Bridge Steam Museum has always concentrated on the theme of work in action, and acts as a major restoration centre for other museums' projects. Also on display is a working forge, where a professional blacksmith forms part of the museum team. The museum holds regular special attractions on site, including a popular steamboat show, and occasional steamings of traction engines. The abiding memory of a visit to Kew Bridge Steam Museum is that of proximity to the genius of West-Country engineering, and to the dizzy experience of climbing and descending the cylinder and beam floors beside the 90 and 100 inch engines.

At the opening of Canbury Gardens, Kingston, 1890

ket town in Medieval times, due to its strategically important position on the river. Until the construction of Putney Bridge in 1729, further up the river, Kingston Bridge was the first crossing point over the Thames above London Bridge. A watercolour by Thomas Rowlandson of about 1800 (now in the museum's collection) shows Kingston's 12th-century timber bridge alongside Bucklands Wharf, where grain and other cargo was unloaded

A selection of Martinware

from sailing barges onto horse-drawn carts. The water-logged remains of the approach to this bridge have recently been discovered by archaeologists, and offer a reminder of Kingston's dependence on the river for its living. Right up to the 1920s and '30s, the heyday of Kingston's river trade, when there were 20,000 licensed watermen, the river was full of working tugs or sailing barges transporting timber, coal, beer, or house-bricks.

The Thames is now much quieter here, the bustling commerce of a working river having mostly gone, although boat building and repair are still carried out. The museum preserves this part of the town's history in photographs, and an important archive collection (including King John's Charter of 1208). Archaeological holdings are particularly important to the museum, which has displays of Anglo-Saxon and Bronze Age material. The redevelopment and new road schemes in the town have meant an influx of new archaeological material into these collections over the past decade, when the

character and face of the town have substantially changed.

It is the museum's role to record and illustrate these radical changes, and in a small upper gallery, and on the ground floor, there are displays relating to Kingston's local history. The archaeological evidence is cleverly related to modern paintings of the sites, although the eerie remains of a Saxon grave will probably grab the first attention of a visitor. The museum was established in 1904 in one wing of the public library, and it still has something of the quiet 'academic' atmosphere of a reading room. The local displays are notable for a small but well-chosen collection of Martinware art pottery (which can also be seen, for example, at **Pitshanger Manor Museum**), and regularly-changing displays of local paintings.

The outstanding gallery in the museum is that devoted to Eadweard Muybridge (1830–1904), who had an internationally famous reputation as a photographer of movement, and played an important role as one of the pioneers of cinematography. Muybridge was born in Kingston, and though most of his working life was spent in America, he returned home to his native town and died in Kingston. The new exhibition gallery is well laid out, with a sequence of fully-illustrated narrative panels and accompanying objects. The dramatically-lit interior forms a contrast in mood and technique to the library-like feel of the rest of the museum. The collection at the museum is of particular importance because it was the personal bequest of Muybridge himself. The material includes his famous zoopraxiscope – the first moving-picture projector – as well as lantern slides, scrapbooks of newscuttings, and an important album of early movement photographs. The changing levels, and the ramped route through the gallery, are intentionally steep, reminding us that Muybridge worked as a photographer until 1881 in San Francisco, a city renowned for its dramatic hills and terraces.

The panels include some of Muybridge's most famous photographs, notably the dramatically-beautiful Falls

of the Yosemite from Glacier Rock in California's national park. Other photographs of the West Coast of America were made under contract to the American government. In the 1870s Muybridge became interested in the photography of moving horses, resulting in the book, *The Attitudes of Animals in Motion* (1881), which revealed a very detailed analysis of the horse in all phases of movement. These photographs, and others of animal and human motion, were quickly recognised as an original and literal study of subjects moving at speed, and they remain one of the best-known sequences of Victorian photography today. Muybridge developed the project into motion photography by his invention of the zoopraxiscope which enabled audiences to see for the first time sequences of pictures as a moving image. The work was continued with intensive photographic sequences of *Animal Locomotion* (1887), building on Muybridge's international reputation as one who had 'laid the foundation of a new method of entertaining the people'. The museum display is completed by an audio-visual presentation of Muybridge's animal locomotion sequences, which recalls the excitement and wonder of the 19th century performances.

Eadweard Muybridge, Sacree Reserve, Canada North-West Territories

Leighton House Museum

*12 Holland Park Road, London
W14 8LZ 01-602 3316*
⊖ High Street Kensington,
Holland Park
Closed Sundays. ⬛
♿ **AG**: stairs to upper floors, no
lift; phone in advance and porters
will assist.
▮ & ♚ guided tours for parties of
not more than 25 by arrangement;
children under 16 must be
accompanied by an adult. ☺

Frederic, Lord Leighton (1830–96),
one of the most renowned High Victorian painters, built his studio-house in
artistic Kensington, lived and worked
there for over thirty years, and eventually bequeathed it to his sisters.
They, 'being desirous that it should be
maintained for the benefit of the public
as a centre of Art, Music and Literature' appointed Trustees in 1896, and
eventually (in 1926) made a gift of the
house to the Royal Borough of Kensington (now Kensington and Chelsea).
The museum has benefitted the public
ever since, and is one of the most
colourful and spectacular buildings in
London's museum community.

   Leighton House was designed for
Leighton by his friend George Aitchison, and built from 1864–66; it ex-
presses, to the very last detail, the
artist's particular taste. The house fulfilled three important functions: those
of a professional work space, a gallery
for the artist's important fine and decorative art collection, and a home.
Leighton's domestic needs were precisely laid down, and rather spartan, as
the original plan shows only one bedroom. His prime concern was his art,
and the first-floor painting studio lies
at the centre of the house.

   The interior of Leighton House,
now sensitively restored, is astonishing
for its richness and artistic vision. The
Inner Hall, with deep-blue William de
Morgan tiles, leads through an anteroom to the wonderful Arab Hall (colour plate 17). This was designed by

Garden view, exterior of Leighton House, 1880

Aitchison, and reflects his understanding (and annotation) of Moorish
architecture. The Arab Hall is based
on a banqueting room of a Moorish
palace in Palermo. The lavish series of
tiles form part of a collection amassed
by Leighton and other scholars, and
vary in date from the 13th to the 17th
centuries, and in place of manufacture
from Damascus to Rhodes. At the
centre of the Hall, a solid block of
black marble is used to create a pool,
reflecting light from the dome above.
Leighton's friends also added specific
decorative touches to the design of the
Hall: Walter Crane, for example, was
responsible for the mosaic frieze.

   The newly-restored library leads off
the anteroom to the Arab Hall, as does
the Drawing Room, which, like other
rooms in the house, was used to display
Leighton's painting collection – here
his French works by Daubigny and
Corot. The wallpaper in the room is
modern, though it is as close as possible to Leighton's original choice
(which was described, rather clubbish-
ly, as 'the colour of the tobacco of a
good cigar'), and redrawn from photographs. Very careful work has gone
into the standard of restoration in other
parts of the room, the silk curtains also
based on photographic evidence, and
the Murano glass chandelier virtually

identical to the one actually owned by
Leighton.

   The Dining Room – where Leighton entertained his fellow artists and
professional colleagues from the Royal
Academy of Art – displays De Morgan
pottery, and further examples of pots
by De Morgan and his followers are
shown in a case on the stairs to the first

Leighton, Corinna of Tanagra, *c. 1893*

Lord Leighton's studio, 1895

Livesey Museum

682 Old Kent Road, London
SE15 1JF   01-639 5604
⊖ & ⇌ Elephant and Castle (2 miles away)
Closed Sundays. ▣
& **GT**: stairs to upper floor – warders will assist.
⋔ & ⋔ book in advance ◉

Sandwiched rather surprisingly between a fast-food restaurant, a church, and a garage, along the busy Old Kent Road in the historic borough of Southwark, is one of London's most innovative small museums, the Livesey Museum.

In 1891 Sir George Livesey, a well-known philanthropist, gave the red-brick building as a public library to the local people of Camberwell and Peckham. The building was damaged in bombing raids in the Second World War, and was eventually reopened by the poet Sir John Betjeman in 1974, specifically as a gallery for temporary exhibitions. Today the museum has built up a reputation for shows that are highly regarded by the local population, heavily visited by school parties, and awaited with keen interest by people all over London. One major exhibition, and one more low-key show, are currently held each year.

floor. Their rich, red-glazed colour and bold animal motifs form a good accompaniment to the colours and patterns of the whole house. The landing on the first floor, known as the Silk Room, was designed by Aitchison as a top-lit picture gallery, intended as a sort of shrine to paintings given to the artist. Of the original collection, Millais's 'Shelling Peas' has recently returned on loan, and paintings by Leighton himself are also displayed there.

The raison d'être of the house is the great studio, where Leighton worked, surrounding himself with a clutter of paintings, fabrics and other objects. Like a number of Victorian artists, Leighton used beautiful objects around him to inspire and encourage his painting. Contemporary photographs (reprinted in the beautifully-produced colour catalogue available at the museum) show a profusion of paintings, casts of sculpture, and furniture in an opulent arrangement.

Leighton added a Winter Studio at the east end of the house in 1889, and this elegant glass and iron structure is now used as an exhibition gallery.

Leighton House was renowned in the artist's time for his impressive series of musical evenings and concerts. Major performers such as Joachim and Charles Hallé, and Clara Schumann, all gave concerts here, no doubt to the rapturous reception of a crowded audience of artists, critics and friends. The tradition has been continued in the museum with a lively musical programme.

A visit to Leighton House succeeds on a number of levels: as a panorama of Leighton's own painting and that of his contemporaries, such as Burne-Jones and Watts; as an exploration of the taste of a leading figure in the Aesthetic Movement; and as a suberb example of the display of an imposing collection of Islamic tiles in a unique architectural setting. The gardens behind the house form a peaceful location for some dramatic sculptures, such as Leighton's own momentous piece, 'Athlete struggling with a Python', of 1877.

Women's Day Trip, c. 1930

One of the features of life along the Old Kent Road is a special style of fast, and occasionally roguish driving, and visitors who cross the road to get to the museum are encouraged to take particular care. In the entrance lobby of the museum the visitor will pass by a bold and lively picture called 'Thames', painted in 1980 by the local artist, Grace Golden. A vital and bustling scene of river life, it is a vivid reminder of the importance of the Thames to the community in north Southwark, where river trades played such an important part in local employment. The working and domestic lives of people in Southwark have played a key part in the exhibition programme of the museum.

The exhibitions originated by the Livesey, especially in recent years, have been characterised by a careful integration of objects from museum collections with purpose-built reconstructions or, most popularly, interactive displays. The exhibition, 'Robots and Automata' in 1986-87, drew national television publicity for its entertaining approach to the subject of mechanical toys and robots, many of which were to be seen scurrying across the two floors of the museum followed by groups of fascinated children. The front entrance of the museum was surrounded by a magnificent twenty-foot-high robot model (nicknamed 'Zark'), designed by Jan Pieńkowski, the author of the children's pop-up book 'Robot'. The model itself was decorated by local schoolchildren, and features in the museum's exhibition poster (colour plate 15), which, like the exhibition itself, was widely acclaimed.

So, too, was 'Light at the Livesey', the 1987–88 show, which concentrated on telling aspects of the story of light. The display used a wide variety of historic objects, such as Roman oil lamps and Victorian gas fittings, to explain the influence and profound effect of natural and artificial light, and included sculptures made by visually disabled people for visitors to touch. The museum ran one of its very popular series of special children's activities, using the local Blackfriars photography project for pin-hole photography workshops. It is always worth finding out

Pinhole camera workshop, 'Light at the Livesey' – 'The Nightmare'

about the activities that accompany each special exhibition, some of which are held in the attractive back courtyard of the museum. Future exhibitions on 'Sport' and 'Rubbish' are planned.

Many objects on show in the Livesey's exhibitions are taken from the fascinating and important museum also run by the London Borough of Southwark, the *Cuming Museum*. This shows a mixed collection of local historical and archaeological material gathered together by R. and H.S. Cuming between 1782 and 1902. It includes important local material, such as the Marshalsea Pump (from the

infamous Debtors' Prison), mentioned by Dickens in *Little Dorrit*, and 'Billies and Charleys' – small lead figures made as fake 'antiquities' by two London labourers, William Monk and Charles Eaton. There is also a particularly interesting display of London superstitions, the Lovett Collection of charms and amulets.

The Borough also runs the *South London Art Gallery*, which has an impressive record of temporary exhibitions of contemporary visual art. This Gallery curates the Borough's important collection of paintings, drawings and prints by British artists, which can be seen on application to the Keeper.

The London Toy and Model Museum

21 Craven Hill, London W2 3EN
01-262 7905/9450
⊖ Lancaster Gate, Paddington,
Queensway ⇄ Paddington
Closed Mondays, except Bank
holidays. ▯▢ & S
▥ & ▥ book at least 14 days in
advance (write for booking form).
◎ Birthday parties catered for
between Tuesdays and Saturdays.

This is one museum that you can hear
at a distance. For if you approach the
London Toy and Model Museum by
foot, the sound of children playing in
the extensive back garden is enough to
alert you to this museum's popularity.
And it must be one of the very few
museums in the world to have a
locomotive in the front garden.

The delight and enthusiasm that the
museum brings is succinctly expressed
in the appreciative children's letters
posted on the pillars in the Clockwork
Cafe, which looks out over the
recently-extended garden. It's a good
place to get a feel of this noisy, informal, and thoroughly entertaining
museum – especially with a piece of
very good, home-made chocolate cake.
Children will probably want to move
straight out to the attractively laid-out
garden, which features a children's
railway over a boat pond, a loco-shed,
and another miniature railway track

circling around a picnic area and an
Edwardian children's roundabout. A
ride-on train in the garden is usually
steam-operated on Sundays.

There are many delights, too, in the
museum itself, which features
commercially-made toys and models,
from the 18th to the 20th centuries. It
is an extremely diverse, colourful, and
comprehensive collection, arranged on
the ground and lower floors of the two
Victorian houses that form the
museum. The collection has been built
up in the belief that childhood memories are particularly important, and that
future generations should have the
chance to enjoy looking at modern and
historic toys. But the museum also has
a tradition of bringing these toys to life
through a well-established and highly-
popular series of special events. There
are open model-steam railway days in

the spring, toy fairs, and an annual
model-boat regatta in the summer,
along with the well-known Teddy
Bears picnic in July. The programme
of special exhibitions also adds to the
museum's appeal, and encourages the
return visits that children invariably
seem to demand after coming to the
museum. As one child summed it up in
a thank you letter to the curator,
'Yesterday's outing to the museum was
brilliant'.

There is plenty to see, since the
cases that fill the small galleries (each
with a particular theme or group of toys
and models) are crammed full of objects, and wall spaces are covered with
posters. Each particular collection
seems enormous in size, from armies
of tin or lead soldiers, to a massive
group of dinky toys, shown with plastic
and tin road vehicles. Transport is a

Some of the museum's teddy bears

Britain's Walking Race (British-made clockwork toy, c. 1890)

Exterior, with the locomotive, 'Witch'

London Transport Museum

Covent Garden, London WC2E 7BB
01-379 6344
⊖ Covent Garden, Leicester Square ⇌ Charing Cross
Open daily. 🚻 🖬
♿ 🅵 WG: special arrangements for groups.
🚼 & 🚼 special facilities: contact Group Visits Department.

Covent Garden, in the City of Westminster, has had a long and varied history. It was the convent garden for Westminster Abbey, and a piazza in the 16th century (designed by Inigo Jones), with the famous fruit and vegetable market established on the site in 1670. This market moved to Vauxhall, south London in 1974. The original market buildings were restored, and the London Transport Museum set up – somewhat incongruously, but to very great effect – in the old wholesale Flower Market. Covent Garden today is both a major shopping centre and a great cultural attraction. The free music and entertainment performed in front of the Inigo Jones-designed St Paul's Church (commonly called the Actor's Church) is a colourful feature of life here. The Royal Opera House, the Photographers Gallery and the new **Theatre Museum** are all close by, making this one of the liveliest and most cosmopolitan parts of London.

The London Transport Museum has a significant part to play in all of this entertainment, and the bustle and clamour of visitors to the area is repeated, happily and noisily, inside this well-attended and much-loved museum. It is an excellent museum for a family visit, even if the history of urban transport doesn't immediately sound like an entrancing idea. The fine cast-iron and glass Victorian building is a draw in itself, giving a feeling of space and light to the major collection of vehicles. It was designed by William Rogers and built in 1871–72 by William Cubitt & Co.

The secret of the museum's success lies in the way that the history of London's transport (which it takes as its grand theme) is treated: the museum considers the effects of transport on human life. The story is a

continuing theme throughout the museum, with a special display on fire engines, and a fascinating train room that has examples of both engines and rolling stock, such as the famous 'Royal Scot' and its coaches (by Basset-Lowke), or the clockwork floor train, 'London', built by the Hess Company in Germany. The best form of motion, to my mind, was supplied by the German Swimming Dog (made about 1900), with a determined and slightly manic appearance.

Other important collections include the exhibition of Paddington Bears, with all manner of bears clothes, and puppets from the television series. This is complemented by a dolls gallery, which takes a historical view from early-18th-century examples to fashion-conscious dolls of the 1950s. Collectors will probably be keenly interested in the reconstructed shop displays, and there are numerous examples of toys manufactured all over the world.

Boats, 'planes, cars, tin toys, games, toy menageries, dolls, dolls' houses, trains, teddy bears, penny toys, model soldiers – the list of things to see in one of London's best small museums seems endless. The museum is suitable for the casual visit, or as a venue for a more organised school group. There is a particularly good museum shop (selling toys, souvenirs and books) in a museum that offers an entertaining visit for children and adults alike.

Women conductors, early 20th century

London Transport poster, 1934

Architects' drawing of new Park Royal station, Ealing, 1935

social one, not merely a mechanical one, though the rich collection of trains, trolleybuses, motor and horse buses, and railway vehicles will certainly appeal to transport enthusiasts and specialists. All around the museum are colourful reminders of the fact that London transport has been, and always will be, a human story. Particularly enjoyable are the displays from the museum's very important collection of posters. London Transport has always set very high standards of graphic design, and some of the 1920s and 1930s advertising posters are classics in their own right. Poster designs are available as postcards from the excellent museum shop at the entrance to the museum.

The social context is also provided through small temporary exhibitions on historic aspects of London's transport history, as well as contemporary issues like the rapid development of the Docklands Light Railway. There are a number of well-written and presented videos around the museum, which consider some 'technical' subjects (like traffic congestion) or, a particular favourite, the recollections of people who worked on the London Buses during the First World War. There are also well-laid-out information panels,

photographs, models, and tickets illustrating the complex changes both in London's transport and in the very shape of London itself. But at the heart of the collection are, naturally enough, the vehicles, many distinguished by the bold, and immediately recognisable colour of London Transport red.

The earliest vehicle on display is in fact a reconstruction – but a very high quality one – of the 1829 Shillibeer Horse Omnibus, a coach that had the distinction of providing London's first regular horse bus service. This vehicle

is an historic item in its own right, built in 1929 to celebrate the London Omnibus Centenary Celebrations. It took some time for the idea of a motor bus to become generally acceptable in London, and it was not until 1910 that the B Type Motor Bus was introduced to the transport system. This was the first mass-produced bus in the world. Many buses of this type were used for troop transport in France and Belgium during the First World War.

Numerous displays in the London Transport Museum are interactive. You can try out the dead man's handle in a tube train, and the simulator of a journey on the underground giving a driver's view of the Circle Line, is especially popular. Impressive, too, is the way that visitors can see the usually unseen sights, under, inside, over, and even through the tubes, trains, and buses. The London Transport Museum is a museum with a canny knack of answering questions about London's great history of public transport in a lively, bold, and imaginative way. It has a reputation of being something of a pioneer amongst London's museums, with a particularly important education department.

A knifeboard car of the North Metropolitan, c. 1888

The Museum of London

London Wall, London EC2Y 5HN
01-600 3699
⊖ Barbican (closed Sundays), St
Paul's, Moorgate, Bank
Closed Mondays. **F** ▣ Coach
parking available.
🚗 **WG**: contact ext. 280 for details
of road access and parking.
🚼 & 👥 must book in writing at least
three months ahead; information
and booking forms by post from
Education Department. ◎

The Museum of London stands in the
heart of the City of London. It is the
capital's premier history museum, and
indeed one of the best museums in
Britain. It combines a simple, dramatic,
and effective chronological layout with
the display of stunning collections telling the story of London and Londoners from prehistoric times to the present day. The Museum of London has
been housed in its current purpose-
built premises on the edge of the Barbican development since 1976, formed
from the collections of the Guildhall
Museum and the London Museum at
Kensington Palace. Given the rapid
changes in London's own architectural
and social landscapes over the past
decade, it is highly appropriate that the
museum itself is now situated in an
area of considerable building activity.
The face of this part of London will be
changed radically over the next decade,
and the museum is itself looking not
only to record the changes brought
about by redevelopment, but also to
increase the number of its own galleries to enlarge on the story of life in the
capital. It is a major opportunity, and
one, no doubt, that the Museum of
London will grasp skilfully and imagi-
natively.

There is a mood of confidence and
friendliness about this museum, which
soon transmits itself to the visitor. The
attendant staff are courteous and helpful, the museum has been designed to
make the visit stimulating not tiring,
and members of the public can often
be seen looking very carefully at the
attractive displays, or reading object

Paul Sandby, Mop Sellers, *1759*

labels with particular attention. It is a
museum that evokes a very real sense
of the city, and of the people living and
working in it; history is made both
intelligible and entertaining.

The story begins with Prehistoric
and Roman times, using the museum's
massive collection of material from
archaeological excavations. Straightforward displays of objects are complemented by impressive reconstructions of a Roman kitchen and dining
room, and the spectacular mosaic
pavement discovered in Bucklersbury
in 1869.

The Medieval gallery displays some
outstanding objects from its major collections – Saxon jewellery, pottery,
coins, and weapons. The timespan of
this section of the museum moves from
'Dark Age London' in the 5th century
to the vigorous 15th-century capital,
and the displays look at all aspects of
life from glamour and pageantry to
poverty and disease. Reconstructed
room settings give more of a human
dimension to the historical narrative,
and some of the fine pilgrim badges on
show attest to the skill of medieval
artists.

The Tudor and Stuart Galleries also
play on the contrast between good and
bad fortune, poverty and prosperity in

London life of the 16th and 17th centuries. The display of the Cheapside
Hoard, discovered in 1912 under a
cellar floor in Cheapside, shows the
splendour of Elizabethan jewellery and
the glamour of courtly life. The Great
Fire of 1666, which destroyed four-
fifths of the city, and the bubonic
plague of 1665, which killed many
thousands of Londoners, were terrible
moments in the capital's history that
are chillingly caught by the popular
audio-visual programme recreating the
Great Fire, and the display of a plague
bell (rung to announce the corpse collector). The Museum's newest gallery
is devoted to 18th century London, and
uses a rich variety of objects and
displays to illustrate domestic and social life of the period – from the grim
reality of a sentence in Newgate Prison, to music-making in Vauxhall Gardens.

The galleries that tell the story of
modern London also use the highly
successful techniques of reconstructed
room or shop settings, and the integration of very diverse collections. The
influence of the Industrial Revolution
on the city is recorded by important
collections devoted to working life.
Major themes of transport and education, in a city with a rapidly expanding
population, are also considered. There
are some fine individual displays: the
Art Deco lifts from Selfridges in Oxford Street (colour plate 22) are a
decorative extravaganza from a store

Late 14th century Pilgrim Badge
commemorating Becket's return from exile

that emphasised shopping as an art form; the reconstruction of a 1930s Woolworth's counter (with an advertising board proudly proclaiming that nothing is sold over sixpence) marks the impact of popular trading.

Port of London Authority policemen testing lifejackets at West India Docks, c. 1930

The Museum of London's collections are of outstanding importance to the history of London, and cover all aspects of life and work in the capital. Items from the major holdings of costume and textiles, and of paintings, prints and drawings, are also woven into the displays. The museum has a high reputation for the quality of its temporary exhibitions, which often show material not displayed in the permanent galleries. The education services are extensive, and specialist lecture series, or the impressive early-evening film programmes are recommended.

As part of the Museum's own development plan is a well-advanced scheme to create the *Museum in Docklands*. This will tell the story of London as a major port and commercial centre. Open days and special events are held at the museum's visitor centre, at the Royal Victoria Dock in east London (otherwise open by appointment only).

Museum of Mankind

(The Ethnography Department of the British Museum)
6 Burlington Gardens, London
W1X 2EX   01-437 2224 ext. 8043
⊖ Piccadilly, Green Park, Oxford Circus
Closed Sunday mornings. **◨**
♿ **XG**: some difficulties for wheelchair users – assistance can be given by warders; limited disabled car parking available – prior booking necessary, phone ext. 8062; information leaflet available from Information Desk or by post from Education Service.
🚻 & 🚼 pre-book all parties over 10 people by phone, well in advance. Free film shows. Schools' Room may be booked for lunch periods, video shows or study sessions – contact Education Service.

Tucked away in Burlington Gardens, in the very centre of London, is the Museum of Mankind, one of the most popular and entertaining museums in

Shadow puppet from Java (Raffles Collection)

the capital. It is housed in a grand building designed in 1866–67 by Sir James Pennethorne to provide premises for London University, and its academic pretensions are denoted by the dignified range of statues on the façade. Inside, the building maintains an elegant and serious character, not unlike that of a London club or learned society. It is an appropriate historical atmosphere for the museum, a reminder of the days when pioneering exhibitions were promoted in London by the societies whose expeditions would return from far-flung corners of the world with new knowledge and extraordinary collections of material.

The Museum of Mankind is the ethnographic department of the British Museum. When Sir Hans Sloane made his founding bequest, which led to the creation of the British Museum, there was a significant proportion of ethnographical material. This collection has been developed into the national collection devoted to non-Western societies and cultures – material from the indigenous peoples of Africa, Australia and the Pacific Islands, North and South America, and parts of Europe and Asia.

The museum has three permanent displays: 'Treasures from the Collections', 'An introduction to the collections', and 'Turquoise Mosaics from Mexico'. In addition, the museum presents several major thematic exhibitions, which look at aspects of a country's culture, or depict the ways of life of particular peoples. The recent exhibition, 'Madagascar – island of the ancestors', for example, considered a country with a very varied range of geographical and climatic features, to demonstrate the beliefs and customs of its population, as well as the appearance of its landscape; the 'Living Arctic' display (on view until 2 July 1989) looks at the contemporary lifestyle and history of the Indian and Inuit peoples of northern Canada – the hunters and trappers of that sparcely-populated part of the Americas.

The standard of the museum's displays is always high, as befitting a collection of such magnitude and historical importance. The holdings that

Easter Island statue, Hoa-Haka-Nana-la, *collected from Orango village, 1868*

the Museum of Mankind draws on to create these exhibitions, and to bring together themes of people, time and lands, are unrivalled in size and scope. They document not only cultures, but also British history. Many objects were originally brought back from pioneering early expeditions, such as Captain Cook's voyages. Other collections were put together by British colonial officers: there is, for example, a particularly important group of shadow puppets and masks assembled by Sir Stamford Raffles, the 19th-century Lieutenant-Governor of Java. The latter collections reflect to some extent the need

for the administrators of the British Empire to understand, document, and use the art and artefacts of colonial countries.

The museum's holdings include some fabulous Mexican mosaics, like the turquoise Aztec-period mask possibly representing the god Quetzalcoatl (colour plate 12), and other stunning items like a Tahiti mourner's costume worn to instil terror in the community on the death of a chief. Sometimes exhibits are created in the galleries themselves for specific exhibitions: a colourful and massive rice barn, for example, was built by Torajan craftspeople for a display on the rice-barn carvers of Indonesia. There are artistic works in the collection along with everyday tools, implements, weapons, and religious items, which illustrate human values and beliefs across the world. The museum's contemporary collecting programme ensures that objects from societies that have been radically changed in this century are saved and explained.

Torajan Rice Barn built in the museum

Museum of the Moving Image

South Bank, London SE1 8XT
01-928 3535
⊖ Waterloo ⇌ Waterloo
Closed Mondays. 🔊▣ ♿ XG
🚹 & 🚺 phone Education
Department in advance.

Any institution that claims to be 'the world's most exciting cinema and television museum' has to be special indeed. Described by one witty, if less than enthusiastic critic as 'a building with all the elegance of a stack of front-loading washing machines', the museum sits underneath Waterloo Bridge in the middle of the extensive South Bank arts complex.

The museum may lack architectural dignity, and the entrance through a very narrow ticket barrier may be unnerving, but once inside, the experience is unforgettable. The first object, a huge model of a human eye, stares impassively towards the entrance steps, at its centre a facetted globe of tiny, fast-moving screen images. It is a fitting symbol for the whole museum experience, where the visitor will be bombarded with pictures, posters, stills, captions, and huge set-constructions. All of these features are contained in a long, chronological

Ceiling of the 'Temple of the Gods'

Mrs Thatcher in her kitchen

narrative, telling the complicated and fascinating history of the development of moving images. Every major aspect of the story, from shadow plays – the world's first moving images, right through to today's high-technology satellite pictures, is covered in a colourful and fast-moving spectacle. There is a special emphasis on the history of British cinema and television, although the collection and displays look at themes that are worldwide.

The first sequence of galleries is devoted to some of the major discoveries in creating effective images – optical instruments such as the Zogroscope, the camera obscura, and the magic lantern. In one darkened room, on a suitably cold floor, there is an alarming reconstruction of the Fantasmagorie, where the visitor can stand behind an 18th century audience watching the grotesque and macabre images, and listen to a diabolic sound-track produced by this application of the magic lantern. Each bay in the sequence takes a theme or subject, and describes the background in some detail. Several

extraordinary early experiments are presented, such as Etienne-Jules Marey's cumbersome 1882 photographic gun, firing twelve images per second.

In this museum the whole style of presentation is to make the visitor learn through make-believe. In the small gallery on the theme 'Cinema goes to War', you will have to look through 'real' periscopes in a trench to see contemporary film of tanks rolling through no-man's-land. One of the best set-pieces in the museum is the 'Temple of the Gods', with six statues of great film stars (Mary Pickford, Buster Keaton, and Theda Bary amongst others) supporting a roof and pediment decorated with a galaxy of screen idols.

There are very popular exhibits at the top of the stairs: a full reconstruction of a 1919 Russian railway carriage (the MOMI Agit train, colour plate 24) with extracts of 'agitprop' and Soviet silent cinema on show; and an unnerving bay dealing with Salvador Dali and Luis Bunuel's surreal film 'Un Chien Andalou'. The visual delights of the museum seem to increase in scale and grandeur from this moment in the tour and the huge reconstructed 1930s film set and cinema foyer are triumphs. The way in to the cinema (inspired by London's Muswell Hill Odeon) is guarded by an immaculately-dressed commissionaire, who will politely ask visitors to queue for a moment before

letting them through the cinema doors – one of a series of actors playing contemporary roles, and bringing more of an authentic atmosphere to the visit. Don't be embarrassed, carry on the conversation.

There are evocative images at every conceivable corner throughout the museum, like clips from classic films, or costume from recent movies (including Meryl Streep's cloak from 'The French Lieutenant's Woman'). The section on television has a fine bank of 1950s TV's, and there is a gallery bringing the whole subject of television production and programming up to date. The section on TV and politics is very apt, and cheekily displayed, with a bank of TV screens propping open the reconstructed front door of no. 10 Downing Street, and a window through which one can see the 'Spitting Image' caricature of Mrs Thatcher avidly studying her copy of the *Sun*.

MOMI is a museum that succeeds in making its subject come alive in ways undreamed of by other museums. It offers the visitor many opportunities to get involved in activities, from editing a film to reading a script from an autocue. There will be an ambitious programme of high-quality temporary exhibitions. MOMI is, and should be, a place of historical entertainment set in its social and political context. It is the most adventurous and exciting of London's new museums.

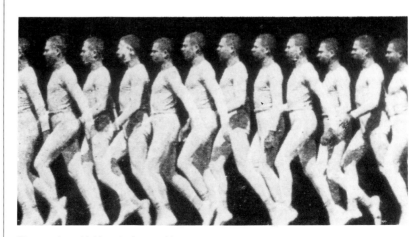

Pictures taken with Marey's photographic gun

Museum of the Order of St John

St John's Gate, St John's Lane, Clerkenwell, London EC1M 4DA
01-253 6644
⊖ Farringdon, Barbican ⇄ Kings Cross, Farringdon
Closed Sundays. ▣
& S: ground floor only.
▥ & ♕ phone Curator in advance.

Any approach by foot to this small yet informative museum will take the visitor through some historic and fascinating parts of London. A journey through Clerkenwell, in the London Borough of Islington, gives one the opportunity to see a range of craft and other small workshops now returning to the area, and it would pay to detour through Smithfield Market (in the City of London), the capital's premier wholesale meat, poultry and game market – an area once renowned for its fairs and tournaments, and also, rather more macabrely, for its executions in the 16th century.

The approach to the museum, housed at St John's Gate, leads the visitor underneath a fine castellated gatehouse. The Gate formed the imposing South Entrance to the Priory of Clerkenwell, completed in 1504 and restored mainly in the 19th century.

The entrance by the Gatehouse leads to the museum displays, and to the major interior rooms of the headquarters of the Most Venerable Order of St John. Staff from the museum regularly lead guided tours around these rooms, and the tours are highly recommended, since the interiors are of considerable architectural and historic interest. The Chapter Hall, with its dignified portraits and imposing oak ceiling, was designed by John Oldrid Scott, and completed in 1903 in the Tudor style appropriate to St John's Gate. Parts of the wooden spiral stairs leading to the library are of early 16th century date, though perhaps the most atmospheric and intimate architecture is to be found in the Crypt, now the only visible part of the original 12th century priory on the site, and one of

London's few existing Norman buildings.

The museum collections at St John's Gate give the story of the Order of St John even more purpose than the surrounding buildings. The Order was essentially religious, founded in the 12th century with a particular emphasis on the care of the sick. The present displays concentrate on telling the story of the Knights of St John and the St John Ambulance. The principal museum room is on the ground floor, by the main foyer, and has had a varied history both as a Stores Department for St John Ambulance and as a robing room for investitures. Today the museum is carefully and systematically laid out, with cases dealing with appropriate themes, such as the Knights Hospitaller, the Military

Knights of St John working in the Order's hospital (detail of book engraving, 1594–1602)

St John the Baptist *panel from the* Weston Triptych, *late 15th century*

Knights, and a particularly interesting section on the Priory of Clerkenwell.

There are some outstanding and beautiful objects in the collection to illustrate an illustrious and chequered story, ranging from paintings, silver, and sculpture to glass and ceramics. Perhaps the most commanding object, given pride of place in the museum, is the haunting panel painting known as the 'Weston Triptych': two surviving wings of a Flemish 15th century altarpiece, which was painted for (or owned by) John Weston, Prior of the Order from 1476–89. The subjects – St John the Baptist (patron saint of the Order), the Presentation of Christ in the Temple, the Trinity, and the Presentation of the Virgin – are characterised by skilful handling of colour, and, in the Presentation in the Temple, some marvellous and intimate studies of people's expressions.

Anna Zinkeisen, Members of St John Ambulance Brigade, *c. 1954*

The second and smaller museum room presents displays showing the history and work of St John Ambulance which was established in 1877 to provide First Aid training, and to supply ambulance material. Much of the collection used to tell this story has come from members and friends of the Order, the Association and Brigade, and emphasis is laid on the devoted service given by volunteers, particularly during the two World Wars. The work of St John Ambulance has its roots in the Hospitaller tradition of the medieval Knights of St John, and provides the museum with an opportunity to look to the future against the background of its historical buildings and ancient site. It is a museum that can be enjoyed at leisure, hidden as it is among the backstreets of Clerkenwell. The visitor who has time to savour a part of London off the beaten track will have a rewarding visit to the museum, and St John's Gate itself.

National Army Museum

Royal Hospital Road, Chelsea, London SW3 4HT   01–730 0717
⊖ Sloane Square ⇌ Victoria
Closed Sunday mornings. 🄵 ◉
🄿 by appointment.   ♿WG
♨ & ♟ book in advance through Education Department (ext. 228).

To find a large military museum in fashionable Chelsea somehow seems a little odd. There is something incongruous, too, about seeing numbers of designer cars on their way to and from the Kings Road passing close to the museum, with its small display of military vehicles parked casually beside the front entrance.

Inside, these contradictions add to the appeal and purpose of the museum. The visitor might reasonably expect the glittering display of military medals; there are around 8,000 in the collection, with a spectacular group of no less than thirty-five Victoria Crosses. Less expected is the telling of the human side to the 'Story of the Army',

and the lively, unusual temporary exhibitions.

Along with the medals is a vast collection of military badges, and, on the second floor of the museum, a changing selection from the world's largest collection of military uniforms. These demonstrate the significant changes in Army dress from the early 'Redcoat' uniform to today's familiar combat dress, or the khaki first used in service in India.

The museum's Art Gallery is arranged in a similar formal and accurate style, with the appearance of a particularly large and prestigious officers' mess. The Gallery displays subjects of military history by renowned artists from the 17th century onwards, including Gainsborough and Reynolds, and well-known Victorian war painters such as Lady Butler. An important recent acquisition is Henry Nelson O'Neil's colourful and sentimental oil painting, 'Home Again'. Many examples from the extensive collection of prints and watercolours are shown in the museum's programme of temporary exhibitions.

These well-attended exhibitions concentrate on diverse and unusual

Wounded soldiers in a temporary dressing station, Boer War, c. 1900

themes, often stressing the human story of Army life. A recent special exhibition, 'Follow the Drum', included a number of the lavishly-decorated drums in the museum's collection, emblazoned with coats of arms or battle honours. The use of audio-visual displays in this exhibition (and the opportunity for visitors to try out their own drum-beating) is typical of the less-than-formal approach to explaining Army history at this museum. Recent museum displays have also included live historical re-enactments.

Telling the history of the British Army – which the National Army Museum has as its main purpose – in an approachable and interesting way is certainly a challenge. It is not, on the face of it, a subject with universal appeal, any more than a transport museum, or a collection of medical instruments. The museum undertakes the task most successfully when it puts the human story at the forefront, and the two sections of 'The story of the Army' on the first floor are the galleries most likely to attract the ordinary visitor.

The first section looks at the early history of the British Army, starting with the formation of the Yeomen of the Guard in 1485, to the outbreak of

Recruits for the Coldstream Guards at kit inspection, c. *1945*

Caricature of army life by James Gillray from The Life of William Cobbett . . . , *1809*

the Great War in 1914. Although there is now an old-fashioned air about this display (which is to be remodelled in the near future), and many of the information labels are exhaustingly long to read, there is no doubting the historical importance of the collections. The work of distinguished Army commanders such as Wellington or Kitchener is covered, and important battles and campaigns also figure prominently. There are proud military relics, such as the Duke of Marlborough's gold-embroidered saddle cloth, and objects captured at the Battle of Waterloo. The mounted skeleton of Marengo, Napoleon's favourite charger (and perhaps the horse he rode at Waterloo), is a rather odd and unexpected display in this academic section of the museum.

The story of the British Army during the period of the First World War and up to the Falklands conflict is the most memorable part of the whole museum, and worth concentrating on if the visitor is pressed for time. There are some impressive and realistic reconstructions of Army life, both in the barracks and engaged in active warfare around the world – from the jungles of Burma in the Second World War, to the fight-

ing at Port Stanley in the Falklands campaign, showing a captured Argentine position on Mount Tumbledown, overlooking Port Stanley. This display is housed in a purpose-built new extension opened in 1983, and incorporates striking audio-visual displays and commissioned models throughout its depiction of a soldier's life. There are also highly accurate dioramas, including dramatic reconstructions of the Battle of Mons in 1914, and the D-Day assault on the Normandy beaches in 1944.

The museum plans to place more emphasis on 20th century collecting, and on exploring, through permanent displays and temporary exhibitions, events within living memory, especially since the Second World War.

The basement of the museum shows a specialist collection of weapons in a rather uneasy and dated gallery, which will shortly be redesigned. This Weapon Gallery traces the development of hand-held weapons from the Middle Ages onwards. The historic collection is accompanied by some grim illustrative material, such as sword-fighting manuals. There are decorative weapons as well as purely functional and deadly arms.

The National Gallery

Trafalgar Square, London
WC2N 5BN   01-839 3321
Recorded information 01-839 3526
⊖ Piccadilly Circus, Leicester
Square, Charing Cross ⇌ Charing
Cross
Closed Sunday mornings. 🄵 🄸
🄳 W: use Orange Street entrance;
ramps and lifts to all floors;
wheelchairs available – phone in
advance.
🚻 & 🚻 contact Education
Department for guided tours and
talks. ◉

National Gallery, the Barry Rooms (built 1872–76)

The National Gallery is without any
doubt one of the world's greatest art
galleries. It houses the nation's collection of Western paintings from the
13th to the early 20th centuries, repre-
senting all the major schools of painting by all the great artists.

More than this, the National Gallery
is one of the small and select group of
museums that can proclaim that all of
their permanent collections are on
show to the public at all times. (The
only exceptions are paintings on tour,
on loan, or undergoing conservation
treatment.) The work of the Gallery
also includes a prestigious temporary
exhibition programme, bringing often
rarely-seen great works from international public and private collections to
London.

Yet the National Gallery manages to
retain a character that if grand is not
pompous, and is comfortable rather
than highbrow. This is due partly to
the well-supported guided tours, which
give an air of learning in action to the
Gallery, and to the regular involvement
of painters and the public in the popular artist-in-residence scheme (where a
contemporary artist is given a studio in
the National Gallery, open to visitors
one day a week). These are all ways of
making famous paintings come alive to
the public, and the National Gallery
feels a dynamic and busy place because
of such programmes. The work of its
education department – organising
video programmes, quizzes, and specialist tours – is outstanding.

As with so many museums, even the
great national ones, the Gallery's holdings developed from a private collection of such importance that public
access to it was considered of para-
mount importance. In 1824 the British
Treasury purchased a group of thirty-
eight paintings from the Russian-born
financier, John Julius Angerstein. The
beginning of a national collection of art
was under way, displayed at first in
Angerstein's own house in Pall Mall,

Titian, Portrait of a Lady, *perhaps c. 1511 (detail)*

but moved to the present site in 1838.
The National Gallery was designed by
William Wilkins, and the fine interiors
that the visitor sees today created by
E.M. Barry (1867–76) and Sir John
Taylor (1885–87). Building has started
on the latest extension to the Gallery,
the new Sainsbury Wing, designed by a
team under the American architect,
Robert Venturi. This will house the
Renaissance and Early Northern collections. Its opening will be one of the
major events in the fine art calendar
this century, equalled by the extraordinary gift in 1985 of a £50 million
endowment fund from J. Paul Getty Jr.
for the purchase of paintings.

Edouard Manet, The Execution of
Maximilian, *c. 1867–68 (detail)*

The recently-restored Barry Rooms
make a good starting-point to a visit to
the National Gallery. They are grand,
elaborate, and meticulously detailed.
The atmosphere here is typical of the
National Gallery as a whole – a mixture
of a railway terminus (full of busy
people) and an old fashioned and luxu-
rious London hotel (with comfortable
seats, marble door-frames, and extravagant wallpaper). The visitor can take
in the fine vistas of the rooms without
disturbing anyone's visual concentration; looking at the paintings themselves in peace will be more difficult,
given the very large numbers of visitors
to the Gallery.

J.M.W. Turner, The 'Fighting Temeraire' tugged to her Last Berth to be broken up, 1838

Peaceful reflection in front of paintings can be found more often in the
lower-floor galleries, where the collection is hung very densely. This is hardly the 'reserve' collection, for the quality of paintings throughout these galleries is very high indeed. It is fair to say
that the upper galleries are used for
more illustrious and famous works –
the paintings renowned throughout the
country. Down in the lower galleries
are less-well-known but equally haunting works, such as the calm and ele-
gantly composed oil by Vincenzo Catena of 'Saint Jerome in his study' (colour plate 13), with the saint's hat cast
onto the floor in his eagerness to get to
his reading, and an inane but friendly
lion fast asleep in the room.

The artists represented in the collection at the National Gallery read like
a roll-call of the best-known and best-
loved painters of all time: Leonardo,
Raphael, Rembrandt, Goya, Monet,
Turner, Constable, and Picasso. The
arrangement of galleries has been
clearly organised, and room plans and
free information leaflets are available
to guide the visitor from the Early
Italian period to the Spanish, British,

or French Rooms, for example. The
leaflet 'A quick visit to the National
Gallery' (available at the superb and
comprehensive shop) can be recommended for visitors who have only a
short time to spare, highlighting sixteen particularly famous works.

The National Gallery provides an
illustrated story of the history of art,
and is justifiably one of the top cultural
attractions in London. There are many
great works to treasure: Constable's
'The Haywain' and 'Salisbury Cathedral', or Gainsborough's evocative portrait of the actress 'Mrs Siddons'. In
the rooms devoted to paintings of the
Dutch school there is a large group of
Rembrandt's work, from self-portraits
to religious pictures. The Spanish
Rooms have powerful paintings by
Velazquez, Murillo, and Goya. Elsewhere, Impressionist works are displayed by Degas, Van Gogh and
Cézanne. One of the most enjoyable
ways of using the National Gallery –
for those who are fortunate enough to
be able to do so – is to come and see
one painting at a time as a sort of
speedy visual tonic, as well as to use it
as a place of artistic discovery.

National Maritime Museum

Romney Road, Greenwich, London
SE10 9NF   01-858 4422
⇌ Maze Hill, Greenwich.
Closed Sunday mornings. 🈂 🖵
🔖 STG
🛇 & 🚻 pre-book only if special
arrangements required (contact
Marketing and PR Department): 🚻
booking form and Education Pack
available from Education Centre.
◎

The National Maritime Museum
houses one of the world's greatest
maritime collections, in a situation of
rural beauty in Greenwich Park. Britain's long history as an island nation is
captured in the museum's extensive
galleries, which can easily fill a day's
visit. The Museum has two principal
sections: the Main Buildings, including
the Queen's House of 1616 (designed
by Inigo Jones), and the Old Royal
Observatory, based in Christopher
Wren's Flamsteed House of 1675.

The full extent and architectural
harmony of the Main Buildings can
best be appreciated from the vantage
point of the Observatory, with its
sweeping views across the Royal Naval

The turret ship Walkure *with an angle of loll*

The stern of the Aquitania

College, through the heart of Greenwich, to the City of London on the
north bank of the Thames. It was here
that John Flamsteed, the first Astro-
nomer Royal, carried out Charles II's
ambition to find out 'the longitude of
places for perfecting navigation and
astronomy.' Flamsteed House today
interprets the story of astronomy and
navigation. The galleries are concerned, for example, with discoveries
of mechanical and electrical timekeep-
ing, showing an outstanding group of
models of the heavens, including examples from the world-famous astrolabe collection. The great feature of
the House is the Octagon Room, which
is virtually unchanged since Wren's
day. The clocks with 13ft long pendu-
lums, behind the wainscot, were used
by Flamsteed himself to check the
regularity of the Earth's rotation.

In the Meridian Building, to the
north of the Observatory, are many
original instruments. The world's
Prime Meridian runs through here;
this location was selected largely because a high proportion of the world's
shipping tonnage was marked with the
Greenwich Meridian.

It is a pleasant five-minute stroll
through Greenwich Park to the Main
Buildings: the 17th century Queen's
House, set in the middle of two elegant

colonnades, which link it to the 19th
century wings. The Queen's House is
currently closed for refurbishment
(due to reopen in 1990). It is noted
particularly for the Great Hall, a perfect cube, and for the first enclosed
courtyard in England, where masques
were held in honour of Charles I and
Queen Henrietta Maria. The interior
of the Queen's Bedroom is unrivalled
for its rich painted ceiling decoration.

Opened on Trafalgar Day, 1986, by
the Princess of Wales, the National
Maritime Museum's gallery, 'Discovery and Seapower 1450–1700', is a
good starting point for a visit. The
gallery starts with a commanding 19th
century oil painting of the great explorer, Vasco da Gama, and includes some
quite breathtaking 17th century ship
models, in a clear, thoughtful, and
slightly opulent display.

There is nothing restrained about
Prince Frederick's Barge of 1732, in
the exhibition room devoted to Royal
Barges on the lower ground floor of the
West Wing. Lit to perfection to show
off its astonishing carved and gilded
decoration, the barge was designed by
the famous architect William Kent for
George II's eldest son, for use on
grand state occasions. It is one of the
most spectacular sights in the museum.

The adjacent gallery, the aptly-

The steam paddle tug Reliant

named Neptune Hall, is impressive for other more workaday reasons. The large gallery contains the strangely marooned paddle tug 'Reliant'. A visit would not be complete without the unnerving experience of walking right through the tug from port to starboard side, where cutaway sections reveal the engine and boiler rooms. Other displays (both below and above the water line of the 'Reliant') explain the development of the steam ship, and there is a lower gallery telling the long history of ports, cargo handling, and shipyards.

The Archaeological Gallery tells a quieter story about the very beginnings of water transport history, from Bronze Age to Medieval times. Great archaeological discoveries, such as the Bronze Age Ferriby Boat (the oldest plank boat in Europe, found, during excavations on the Humber foreshore) are exhibited in imaginative reconstructions. These displays are supported by detailed technical information about the construction of early craft. The Sutton Hoo display records one of the most outstanding finds in British archaeology, centred around the remains of a large open boat, which had undoubtedly been used for the burial of an Anglo Saxon king.

'The Way of a Ship' uses a dramatic centrepiece – a huge reconstruction of HMS 'Cornwallis' of 1813 – alongside six audio-visual presentations concerned with aspects of maritime life aboard a ship of the line. It is a popular gallery, bringing history vividly to life, as do the models and excellent photographs on show in the 'P & O 150th

Anniversary' exhibition by the museum cafeteria. This gives a flavour of elegant sea transport in the days of the British Empire, but is brought sharply up to date through a series of paintings by David Cobb, showing ships from the Peninsular & Oriental Steam Navigation Company at war in the Falklands conflict.

One of the great features of the National Maritime Museum is the oil painting collection. There are splendid formal portraits of great naval figures, including Marcus Gheeraets the Younger's fine depiction of Sir Francis Drake. Drake is renowned for his achievements against the Spanish Armada (he is shown wearing the Armada jewel), and for being the second man to navigate the world (in 1577–80). There are stirring works, too, of naval combat, such as Turner's epic painting of 'The Battle of Trafalgar, 21st October 1805', the final fleet action in the Napoleonic Wars, commanded by Vice-Admiral Lord Nelson.

Nelson gets pride of place in galleries on the first floor of the West Wing, which concern both his and Napoleon's roles in naval warfare. Greenwich in fact became a place of pilgrimage after Nelson's body was brought to lie in state at the Royal Hospital. The museum has on display one of its most important objects, Nelson's undress coat with the tiny hole made in the left shoulder by the musket shot that killed him. The bloodstains on the lining are a telling image of the death of a national hero. The explorer, Captain James Cook, also warrants a gallery devoted to his three long, arduous, and pioneering voyages of discovery.

The National Maritime Museum is a museum that is as much as great explanation of Britain's social history as it is a story of the sea. The 1988 Armada exhibition (held in the East Wing of the Main Buildings) brought international publicity to the museum as a leader not only in the sphere of academic research but also of display. It is a reminder of the central place that a museum can have in the country's cultural life – a great tribute to a great museum.

National Portrait Gallery

St Martin's Place, London WC2H OHE   01-930 1552
⊖ Charing Cross, Leicester Square ⇄ Charing Cross
Closed Sunday mornings. ◨ but charge for special exhibitions.
⅊ S: phone to make arrangements.
ⅈ contact Education Department (ext. 278).

Putting a face to a name, or a name to a face, becomes an art form at the National Portrait Gallery. Here is Britain's Hall of Fame (and, some would argue, infamy), contained in an exceptional and unique collection of portraits of famous British men and women. The overriding first impression is of a huge display of oil paintings, densely hung throughout the three floors and two mezzanine levels of the gallery. But a closer survey reveals that portraits have been captured in many other forms – from stately busts to tiny watercolours, and a fine group of photographs (though these have, rather surprisingly, only been collected systematically since 1968).

The National Portrait Gallery has its origins in a debate in the House of

J.C. Horsley, Isambard Kingdom Brunel, *1857*

Commons in 1845. It was deemed that a new gallery should be established to provide models of instruction, a focus of national pride, and a generous vote of thanks for Britain's role in shaping world history; and on the artistic side, a major boost to the art of portrait painting, and an instruction to students of costume or art historians. As Lord Palmerston pointed out in the Commons' debate: 'There cannot, I feel convinced, be a greater incentive to mental exertion, to noble actions, to good conduct on the part of the living, than for them to see before them the features of those who have done things which are worthy of our admiration, and whose example we are more induced to imitate when they are brought before us in the visible and tangible shape of politics.' This was a heady mix of possibilities: art, history, personality, and morality combined together. It has remained a potent attraction ever since the National Portrait Gallery was opened to the public in 1859, at premises in Great George Street. The collection was moved to a number of other unsatisfactory buildings before William Alexander gifted the current premises in St Martin's Place, to the side of the National Gallery.

The current arrangement of paint-

Dame Barbara Hepworth, Self-portrait, *1950*

ings is skilfully handled by chronology and theme. The top floor groups together portraits from the Tudors to the Regency period, with pertinent sections on themes such as 'The Arts in the 18th Century', or 'The Romantics'. The first floor contains the special exhibition gallery, and covers Victorian and Edwardian Britain. The Upper Mezzanine covers the Middle Ages, and the Lower Mezzanine contains the very popular gallery on the Royal Family, and the 20th Century collections. Special exhibitions are also held here, and the Gallery has a well-earned reputation for its influential support of contemporary portraiture.

Even though the Gallery is displayed with what seems like every inch of wall space covered, only a relatively small proportion of the Gallery's collection of about 9,000 portraits is on view. It is advisable before a visit to make a selection of the rooms that are likely to be of most interest, using the gallery plan. The dense hang makes an extended visit quite tiring. It is certainly worth spending time reading the informative labels beside each work, which name the portrait and summarise the achievements that have brought each person into the official halls of fame.

The display of Rodrigo Moynihan's soft, grey, portrait of Margaret Thatcher at the gallery entrance – opposite the busy (and excellent) shop

Johnny Rozsa, Sade

Studio of Nicholas Hilliard, Sir Francis Drake, *1581*

National Postal Museum

King Edward Street, London
EC1A 1LP   01-239 5420
⊖ St Paul's, Barbican
Closed Saturdays and Sundays. ▣
⚬ **AG**: limited by steps – phone in
advance for assistance.
▥ & ⚏ special arrangements can
be made for visiting after normal
opening hours – written requests
in advance to The Curator. ☺

Postman's Park, off St Martins le
Grand in the City of London, is an
unusual and slightly sombre, but very
moving departure point for a visit to
the National Postal Museum. The park
is now mostly used by office workers
from the City on their hurried lunch-
breaks, sitting on benches under the
powerful gaze of a tense, hunched
sculpture of a Minotaur by Michael
Ayrton. In the park, too, is a memorial
wall of plaques devoted to heroic men
and women who have sacrificed their
lives to save others from harm or in-
jury. Each panel records a tragic deed,
such as that of 'Alice Ayres . . . who by
intrepid conduct saved 3 children from
a burning house . . . at the cost of her
own young life' in 1885. It is a little-
known garden, with a through route to
the imposing building that houses the
museum.

The National Postal Museum is
situated beside the London Chief Post
Office, with an entrance marked by a
splendid green and gilt Victorian post
box. The lower gallery shows extended
exhibitions concerned with the history

Stamp commemorating Coronation of Queen
Elizabeth II

– is a witty touch. The sequence of
political leaders forms a dominant
thread through the collections. There
is a notable study of Winston Churchill
by Walter Sickert, and an imposing
bronze head of Aneurin Bevan by Peter
Lambda, which captures his passionate
and visionary personality. Great figures
of art and literature are also very well
represented: a tiny drawing of Jane
Austen catches her sharp and sensitive
character, while the self-portrait of the
young Gwen John, regarded as one of
the Gallery's finest works, is clearly
expressive of the painter's strong will
and nerve. The portrait of William
Shakespeare, attributed to John
Taylor, has the distinction of being the
first picture that came into the National
Portrait Gallery collection, and the
only portrait that can reasonably claim
to be a genuine likeness of the play-

wright. As well as straightforward portraits of individual men and women,
there are paintings that capture the
atmosphere of larger society gatherings
(such as Alfred Euglie's 'Dinner at
Haddo House', which sums up the
opulence of a Victorian dinner party),
or significant moments of state politics
(the precise and formal oil of 'The
Somerset House Conference' is a particularly appealing painting, recording
the Treaty that brought to a conclusion
twenty years of war between England
and Spain).

Four outstations of the National
Portrait Gallery – Beningbrough Hall
near York, Montacute House in
Somerset, Gawthorpe Hall in Lan-
cashire, and Bodelwyddan Castle near
Rhyl – display portraits from the collection appropriate to the periods of
the properties.

Stamped letter with Exeter postmark, 1842

of post, describing various themes related to postal services, and illustrating them with contemporary objects, models, and photographs. Subjects that have been covered include the Post Office (London) Railway, opened in 1927, describing the workings and management of the underground railway linking sorting offices with the main termini at Paddington and Liverpool Street Stations.

The main feature of the Museum's collection is, of course, the highly important, and huge, reference collection of stamps on display in the main gallery of the museum. Here a bronze cast relief profile of Reginald M. Phillips of Brighton, the founder of the museum, throws a rather eagle-eyed and almost ferocious glance along the gallery. A marble plaque beneath the sculpture identifies Phillips's ambition in donating to the Post Office in 1965 his massive collection of British 19th century postage stamps:

'His object was to create a living tribute to the vital contribution that Britain has made to international postal communications through the development of uniform postage and the invention of the postage stamp'.

This grand and substantial aim is relayed in the museum by two principal means: through the display of perma-

nent collections and through a programme of regular temporary exhibitions.

It is probably the serious student or philatelist who will gain most from a detailed visit to the museum, which holds a collection regarded as one of the most important and extensive in the world. There are unique stamps in abundance here, displayed with due attention to their preservation on pull-out racks. The famous Penny Black,

for example – itself a symbol of Britain's pioneering place in the history of postal communication – is shown in the only surviving complete sheet of 240 stamps, the proof sheet that was taken from the printing plate in 1840, before the print run of what was the world's first stamp.

The Post Office's own collection forms a complementary group of stamps, proofs, original artwork, and three-dimensional objects. It is essentially a prime reference collection of all postage stamps issued by officers under the control of the British Post Office, and includes nearly all stamps issued since the Penny Black in 1840, together with fascinating details, such as original designs and trial stamps. The museum's third major collection is the Berne Collection of stamps from countries belonging to the Universal Postal Union. This is a worldwide collection of major historical importance, and adds to the comprehensive nature of the museum.

The philatelist is well served by these great holdings, as well as the library and research facilities offered by the museum. Those interested in design or social history have their needs met by a practical selection of temporary exhibitions, which look at topical issues, and details of manufacture and communications.

Die proof for George V ten shilling stamp

Natural History Museum
(British Museum [Natural History])

Cromwell Road, London SW7 5BD
01-938 9123
Recorded information 01-725 7866
⊖ South Kensington
Open daily. 🖫 ▣
🕭 **WG**: phone in advance for parking facilities (01-938 9141).
🕴 **F**: book well in advance – contact the Visitors' Resources Section (01 938 9090); Teachers' Centre available to discuss school visits with museum staff.
🕴 Discount. Family centre open during some school holidays. ◎

The Natural History Museum is one of the world's most magnificent museum buildings, and, in its entrance hall, contains one of the great museum views. The Central Hall is a vast cathedral-like space, which is dominated by the early-20th-century plaster cast of the skeleton of the American dinosaur, Diplodocus Carnegii. It is an unforgettable sight, leading to a creative look at the world of natural history. This is a museum with vast collections (numbering around fifty million items) that can, and does, ask and explain profound questions about our life on earth. Although this may make the museum sound like a learned university department, where wisdom is only imparted in scholarly words to grave researchers, nothing could be further from the truth. While the bedrock of the museum's work is its function as an institution of scientific research, its public face is friendly, informative, and seeks to involve the visitor in a journey of discovery.

The Hall of Human Biology is a good place to start this journey. It is a very popular gallery, which uses models and interactive displays to tell the story of human life, and both our mental and physical growth. Hearing the sounds from inside a uterus, in front of a huge model of an unborn baby seven

View of main entrance hall with Diplodocus *skeleton*

months after fertilization, is an unusual museum expeience. The explanation of reproduction, birth and growth is both clear and logical, and the thematic approach to the subject has been welcomed by literally millions of visitors. The use of interactive exhibits, computer games, and numerous video programmes throughout the museum's thematic galleries encourages learning through discovey in a succinct and highly entertaining way.

The museum combines this high-technology approach with displays of historic grandeur. In the exhibition 'Whales and their relatives', the monumental size of whale skeletons, and the huge blue whale, make an astonishing spectacle. The narrative is skilfully written to bring the fate of these huge air-breathing mammals into perspective. Hunting has reduced the world population of some whale species to dangerously low levels, although today's international agreements to protect whales have done much to save them from extinction. Not so lucky was the Steller's Seacow, exterminated in the 18th century.

It was the sheer proliferation of animal species (as well as their disappearance from the earth's surface) that led the great ntural historian, Charles Darwin, to formulate a convincing argument to explain evolutionary change. His theory of natural selection is discussed in the 'Origin of

Species' exhibition, which is bold enough to ask the daunting question, 'Why are there so many different kinds of living things?', and give a clear account of Darwin's conclusions and answers. The display uses models and dioramas, as well as a computer game, to shed light on the way that animals or insects develop inherited characteristics to help them in the art of survival – through camouflage or mimicry, for example.

This is just one of the large-scale exhibitions throughout the museum.

Mary Anning (1799–1847), who found the first complete Ichthyosaurus *skeleton*

There are other, smaller displays which may be suitable for the visitor with limited time, and the prestigious temporary exhibitions are always worth seeing. The video programme in the Central Hall on 'Dinosaurs and their living relatives' is well presented, and fits in with a sequence of exhibits describing the evolutionary link between dinosaurs and present-day reptiles and birds. The reconstruction of 'Claws' is a fascinating account of the discovery by William Walker in 1983 of a fossil in a Surrey claypit, which proved to belong to a previously unknown flesh-eating dinosaur living over 124 million years ago. The model of the dinosaur after its death makes a powerful and haunting image.

Although modern techniques are employed in a significant proportion of the new displays in the Natural History Museum, there are also more formal, scholarly exhibits. These remind us of the museum's highly important work as a research institution, with a staff of scientists engaged in the identification and classification of animals, plants, and minerals, as well as the care of the museum's huge collections. Scientists are grouped into five research departments (Biology, Zoology, Entomology, Palaeontology, and Mineralogy). The arrangement of the Insect Gallery is typical of the displays that use the study collections. It incorporates some large-scale models of great detail, and puts the specimens into context by describing the economic importance of certain species – whether they are destructive or beneficial to humans.

The Natural History Museum contains the national collection of Plants, Animals, Rocks, and Minerals, in a purpose-built gallery designed by Alfred Waterhouse, and constructed between 1873 and 1880. It is a huge hymn of praise in itself to the Victorian ambition to contain and describe the wonders of creation. There are fine vistas – from the upper galleries across the Central Hall, for example, or across the gallery displaying the mineral study collections – and good architectural details. The terracotta mouldings on the main staircase of the central hall, or on the numerous pillars, are works of art in themselves.

This museum is a building of such scale that it would be wise to select a handful of galleries before the visit begins: there are helpful information panels, and a handy mini-guide to the museum, as well as a descriptive colour guide book. The very lively programme of events is listed in a monthly information leaflet. Whatever the visitor's particular interest, from mineralogy to British natural history, from fossils to birds or fishes, one can be sure that the subject will be covered in an informative and stimulating way.

North Woolwich Old Station Museum

Pier Road, North Woolwich, London E16 2JJ   01-474 7244
⊖ Stratford then ⇌ to North Woolwich
Closed Sunday mornings. 🄵
♿ XG
👤 contact Museum Administrative Assistant in advance. 👥 contact Extension Services Officer.

This attractive museum is set, very strategically, at the end of the British Rail North London Link Line. It is surrounded by all manner of transport routes: road, rail, river, and air. Certainly the train journey through a harsh industrial landscape puts the advertising campaign stressing the urban joy of life in London's Docklands into social context. You may pass within a runway's length of the glossy new City Airport, or take the smart Docklands Light Railway to Stratford on your journey to the museum. You will pass through grim London working (and not working) London on the trip.

The end of the line is well worth getting to, and the formation of a museum within the former railway sta-

The blue whale, 'Whales and their relatives' display

A railwaywoman driving an electric platform trolley, First World War

tion building at North Woolwich one of the cultural high-spots on the Docklands map. A listed building, the station was built in the middle of the 19th century in an imposing Italianate manner, reflecting the importance of its position on the Victorian rail network as well as its proximity to Woolwich Pier. The pier was originally owned by the Railway, and handled a busy and profitable river trade.

The museum has been restored to a period when rail travel from this major ferry, river, and rail terminus in east London was at its heyday, around the outbreak of the First World War. It is a friendly and evocative building, with museum 'guards' in Great Eastern Railway uniform happy to help with any enquiries. Inside the museum, with its fine flagstone floors, is a sympathetic and gleamingly-polished display, including train models, signs, plans, memorabilia, and a large colleciton of archive photographs.

The Great Eastern Railway rapidly developed from the end of the 19th century, and connected London with the main towns and ports of East Anglia. The industrial landscape here was punctuated by many branch lines such as this one, serving the local working community. The museum collections bring that past alive. The large size of the Booking Hall reflects the amount of traffic once expected through this busy station. The bold colour scheme of blue, red and gold is

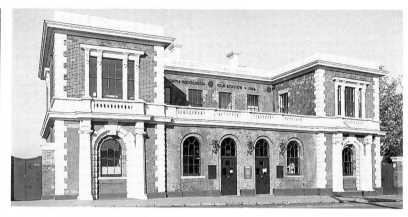

Front view, North Woolwich Old Station Museum

in keeping with the actual colour scheme of Great Eastern Railway exhibits.

The reconstructed Ticket and Parcels Office contains the original wall benches, with additional furniture and equipment taken from the ticket offices at Bethnal Green. Passenger tickets would have been sold here through the office window, and parcels taken in at the counter. The Vestibule, Ladies' and general Waiting Rooms contain railway memorabilia from both the Great Eastern Railway and the London and North Eastern Railway.

The pride and joy of the museum's collection is kept fittingly enough outside, on the turntable – a beautifully-restored Great Eastern Railway steam

locomotive. It is an 0–4–0 'Coffee-Pot' saddle-tank engine, number 229, and is the only survivor of a class of engines that were regularly used to shunt goods trains at Canning Town (further down the line), and to the docks and wharves of east London. In keeping with the consistent period displays in the station, this late-Victorian engine has been restored to a colour scheme and condition of about 1910.

The platform area of the station has a clutter of railway material, from signalling equipment to a two-compartment section of a 1903 London, Tilbury and Southend coach. The museum's display track, which runs parallel to the curent British Rail line, is used on Sundays to display working locomotives in steam. There are ambitious plans to extend the whole project to the adjacent goods yard site, which would become a display area for other large exhibits. The museum also hopes to run a steam-hauled train service from North Woolwich to Silvertown, which would connect the museum directly with the Thames Flood Barrier.

The museum tells an imaginative story of Great Eastern Railway life, and puts the story of railway development into a social context most effectively through the display of contemporary photographs. This is highly fitting historical use of a station that had become redundant to British Rail's needs in 1970.

Booking Hall, North Woolwich Old Station Museum

14   The Library at Kenwood designed by Robert Adam. The Iveagh Bequest, Kenwood.

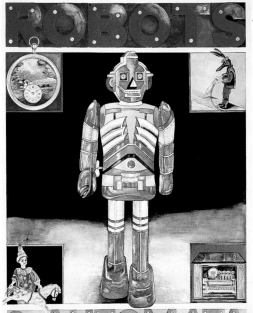

15 *Left   Poster for 'Robots and Automata' exhibition. Livesey Museum.*

16 *Opposite   The Arab Hall, Leighton House. Leighton House Museum.*

17 *Below   19th century Scroll painting from Bengal. The British Museum (on display at the Museum of Mankind in 'Traffic Art: Rickshaw Paintings from Bangladesh' until early 1990).*

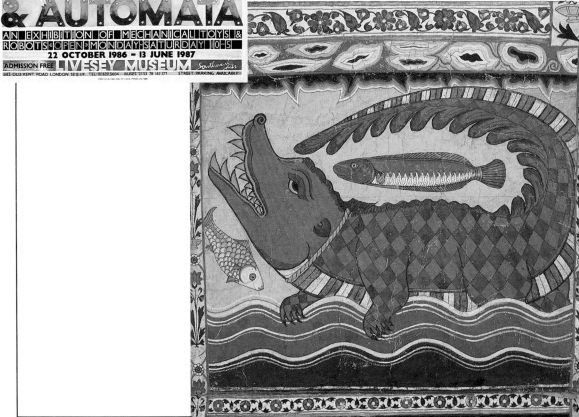

18 Opposite, above   Steam Hammer *by James Nasmyth, 1871. Science Museum.*

19 Opposite, below   London from Greenwich Park *by Jan Vorsterman, about 1680. National Maritime Museum.*

20 Above   Vanitas, *painted by Benjamin Senior Godines in Amsterdam, 1681. The Jewish Museum.*

21 Left   Design by Pierre Fourmaintraux for a stained glass panel to be made by Whitefriars glassworks, probably 1950s. Harrow Museum and Heritage Centre.

22 Below   Lifts from Selfridges department store in Oxford Street, 1920s. The Museum of London.

23 Opposite   Richard Sackville, 3rd Earl of Dorset by William Larkin, 1613. Rangers House (The Suffolk Collection).

*24   Reconstruction of a 1919 Russian
railway carriage with extracts of 'agitprop'
and Soviet silent cinema. Museum of the
Moving Image.*

Orleans House Gallery

Riverside, Twickenham, Middlesex TW1 3DJ   01-892 0221
⊖ Richmond ⇌ St Margaret's, Twickenham
Closed Mondays and every morning. 🅵 🅿
& **W** ground floor, no lift to upper galleries.
♿ & ♦ notify the Curator in advance; talks and guided tours by arrangement.

One of the special features of the museum community in London is the great grouping of historic houses and collections in west London, many of them buildings with riverside walks or views. Orleans House Gallery falls into this category, situated on the banks of the Thames, and in close proximity to *Marble Hill House* and *Ham House*. A trip taking in all three sites forms an enjoyable, artistic, and architectural outing, for as Daniel Defoe wrote in his *Tour thro' the Whole Island of Great Britain* (1724):

'From *Richmond* to *London*, the River sides are full of Villages, those Villages so full of Beautiful Buildings, Charming Gardens, and Rich Habitations . . . that nothing in the World can imitate it.'

Orleans House is situated in a lovely, tranquil river and park setting, with ample opportunity to walk along the tow path to *Marble Hill House* (a complete example of an English Palladian villa built in the 1720s), or to take the ferry across the river to *Ham House* (a remarkable 17th century building set in gardens now replanted in 17th century style).

The Orleans House Gallery is modest in size, and while parts of the interior have rather a 'municipal' feel about their decoration, this only serves as a contrast to the extraordinary internal decor and sculpture of the Octagon. The House started life in the early 1700s as a residence for James Johnston, who had been appointed Joint Secretary of State for Scotland. Johnston added the Octagon (designed by James Gibbs) to the house in 1720,

Interior of the Octagon

reputedly in honour of Caroline, Princess of Wales, wife of George II. The House takes its name from its most famous resident, Louis-Philippe, Duc d'Orleans (King of France from 1830–48), who leased it from 1815–17. Most of the original building was destroyed in the 1920s, although the Octagon survived to be saved through the purchase of the property by Mrs Ionides, who bequeathed it, along with a very important collection of topographical works of art, to the then Borough of Twickenham.

The Octagon itself is the best place to start a visit to the Gallery. The restrained design of the exterior hardly prepares one for the rich decoration, in the baroque style, of the interior. The elaborate sculptural plasterwork was made by two celebrated Swiss plasterers, and the reclining female figures above the chimneypiece may have been designed by the famous sculptor, Michael Rysbrack, who is known to have collaborated with James Gibbs, the architect, on other projects.

When Johnston commissioned the building of the Octagon, he was known to be a particular favourite of the future King George II and his wife, Caroline of Ansbach. Caroline would certainly have been well acquainted with the baroque style of architecture and decoration from buildings in her native Germany, and she must have been particularly at home during entertainments held for her in the Octagon. Contemporary records speak of one party for 'ye Queen and all ye Royal Familie in [the] Octagon in the Garden which is a very fine Rome' in 1729. The banquet for this party sounds as rich and colourful as the interior itself, with capons, oysters, venison, chicken, and lamb all on the menu. No doubt the fresh fruit and vegetables were of the highest standard: John Macky wrote in his *Journey through England* (1711–3) that 'Secretary Johnston . . . has the best Collection of Fruit, of

Pieter Andreas Rysbrack the Younger, A View of Richmond Ferry, *1740*

all sorts, of most Gentlemen in England: His Slopes for his Vines, of which he makes some Hogsheads a year, are very particular, and Doctor Bradley of the Royal Society, who hath wrote so much upon Gardening, ranks him amongst the first-rate Gardiners in England.'

Thomas Rowlandson, Richmond Bridge, *1790s*

Next to the Octagon is a gallery and upper floor used to display temporary exhibitions, and works from the museum's permanent collections. The Ionides Bequest is a particularly important feature of the latter, and forms a major pictorial and historical record of Richmond and Twickenham. Mrs Ionides displayed her collection on the walls of her home at Riverside House, adjacent to Orleans House, and when she bequeathed the works to the Borough she stipulated that the section of the House beside the Octagon should be converted to an art gallery. There are important works in this collection of over 400 paintings, drawings, and engravings. Well-known watercolour painters, including Peter de Wint and Joseph Farington, are represented, and there are oils by 18th century artists such as Samuel Scott, and panoramic views from Richmond Hill. There are also drawings and watercolours of Orleans House itself. The Ionides Bequest is complemented by displays from the Borough's permanent collection of works of art, which includes such important topographical paintings as 'A view of Richmond Ferry' by Pieter Andreas Rysbrack the Younger.

Percival David Foundation of Chinese Art

School of Oriental and African Studies, 53 Gordon Square, London WC1H OPD
01-387 3909
⊖ Euston Square, Goodge Street, Russell Square, Euston
Closed Saturdays and Sundays. ◼
🚾 A
🏛 & 🚻 phone the Secretary-librarian in advance; maximum 20 people; person in charge of group to make themselves known to the porter.

Many cultural visitors to London regard the capital as a place for grand and great artistic experiences, in major West End theatres, or the biggest national museums. But in the heart of London there are smaller and more intimate museums that are well worth seeking out. In fact a 'town trail' around a group of museums such as the *Thomas Coram Foundation for Children*, the *Petrie Museum of Egyptian Archaeology*, the **Jewish Museum**, and **Dickens House** could happily be undertaken on foot and bring the curious visitor into contact with a staggering range of material from varied and disparate cultures. Each of these small

and unusual museums has its own character and charm, resulting from the combination of an interesting building and a prestigious collection. The visitor will often find that the pressure of numbers that will accompany most trips to a larger and substantially more popular museum is relaxed in these quieter surroundings. And the quality of a visit – if it is measured in contemplation and restful viewing – is high for these hidden museums.

The Percival David Foundation of Chinese Art, administered by the University of London, is a fine example of such a museum. The Foundation is home to the wonderful collection of Chinese ceramics given to the University in 1950 by the scholar, Sir Percival David (1892–1964). Sir Percival's gift was intended both to provide the student and researcher of Chinese ceramics with the opportunity to work with an outstanding reference collection of pots, and to inspire a wider interest in China, its history, and its culture. The Foundation expanded this large ceramic collection of around 1500 pots through the addition of works gifted by Mountstuart W. Elphinstone, and together these collections create a great and discriminating survey of Chinese ceramic history from the 9th to the 19th centuries. There is a particular emphasis on Chinese court taste of the 18th century, and a number of the pots are known to have come from the personal collections of

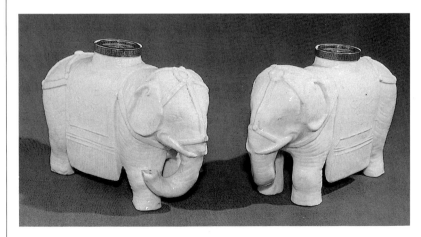

Pair of white-ware elephants with cloisonné flower-holders, Ch'ing, Ch'ien-lung 1736–95

Famille rose vase, mark of Yang-cheng, 1723–35

of the outstanding artistic quality of its collections, but also because the museum has a policy of showing the entire collection on permanent display whenever possible. It is displayed on three floors of what was previously a private house in Bloomsbury, over-looking Gordon Square. There is a comfortable domestic scale to the galleries and the feel of being inside a grand town house adds to the enjoyment of looking at the pots. The displays are systematic, with the Lady David Gallery on the ground floor either having a special temporary exhibition or showing a summary of wares from the whole collection, and the earliest objects on the first floor preceding later porcelains on floors above from the Ming and Qing Dynasties and beyond.

The mood of a visit to the Percival David Foundation was established in my mind by a verse from the poet Chuang Tzu (born 300BC) on display amongst other literary and philosophical quotations:

Fishes are born in water. Man is born in Tao. If fishes get ponds to live in, they thrive. If man gets Tao to live in, he may live his life in 'peace'.

There is something of this reflective and profound belief in the quality of a visit – even a brief one – to the collection. The understated and simple displays make you begin to look for details on the pots. There is little that is declamatory about these wares: each seems to have a quiet and often soothing appeal, so that the eye is drawn to observe small, yet beautiful points of detail. For example, on a 12th–13th century funerary urn of Lonquan

Chinese emperors. Several pieces show poems from the brush of Emperor Qianlong.

Perhaps the best known pieces are the 'David' vases, which have immense historical significance as they are the earliest-known dated examples of underglaze blue-decorated porcelain. There are many other works of similar documentary and technological importance.

The Percival David Foundation is an unusual museum, not only because

Water dropper in form of a buffalo, gold-glazed monochrome, 18th century

Beaker-shaped vase of bronze form with turquoise glaze, Ch'ien-lung period, 1736–95

Celadon (no. 204), the colour of the soft green glaze is appealing in itself, and a rather friendly dragon is curled around the neck of the vase, eyeing a perky bird on top.

Not all of the effective details are of birds, animals or fish, however. An oil-spot bowl of the 11th–12th century (no. 301) is perfection in miniature, the stoneware pot catching the light with little speckles of oil in the glaze. On the third floor there is a breathtaking display of vibrant-coloured wares, from rich copper-red glazes to intense greens and yellows, and, tucked in a corner of a case on the top floor, some serene seated figures of buddha.

This is a good museum, not only as a place to give oneself a visual treat, but also as one to return to and relax in, to see old favourites in a tranquil atmosphere. The displays give the pots space to breathe, so that each object is treated almost with reverence, inviting an unobtrusive rapture for each perfect work of art.

Pitshanger Manor Museum

*Mattock Lane, Ealing, London
W5 5EQ
01-579 2424 ext. 42683*
⊖ & ⇌ Ealing Broadway
Closed Sundays and Mondays. ▣
& **SG**, access to part of the ground floor by ramps.
⚿ & ⚿ phone Museums Officer at least two weeks in advance; guided tours by arrangement.

The creation of Pitshanger Manor Museum is one of the great recent achievements in the world of London museums, and it has opened to both public and professional acclaim.

Pitshanger Manor is intimately connected with the life and career of the architect, Sir John Soane (see **Sir John Soane's Museum**); it was bought by him in 1800 for use as his country villa. The house had previously been enlarged by George Dance, who built a Drawing Room and Eating Room in 1768. Soane had strong memories of that project: 'I was naturally attached [to the house] it being the first whose progress and construction I had attended at the commencement of my architectural studies in Mr Dance's office'. Soane himself made major alterations to the Regency villa, demolishing the oldest part, and building

in its place, beside the George Dance wing, a rectangular four-storey block, with a commanding triumphal-arch façade. Pitshanger Manor was set in a fine and large garden, with 24 acres of grazing land beyond. It provided Soane with the restful atmosphere and the opportunity to experiment with ideas for his town house and museum in Lincoln's Inn Fields.

Soane owned Pitshanger Manor from 1800 to 1810, when family troubles and increasing professional commitments forced him to sell the estate. After a succession of owners, the house was purchased by Ealing District Council in 1900, and opened as a public library; the grounds became a public park. By 1980 the London Borough of Ealing had decided to move the library to new premises, and took the enlightened step of considering a major restoration project for the Grade 1 listed house. That decision led to the creation of the new Pitshanger Manor Museum, in keeping with the Borough's desire to increase access to, and use by, the local community of its public buildings, as well as the spirit of Soane's enthusiasm for museums.

The restoration programme was advanced enough for the Pitshanger Manor Museum to open in 1987, and there are plans for further restoration work to the interior, exterior and grounds. Although the restoration is unfinished, there is still much to see in the museum, and a visit will be en-

One of many early versions of the design for the East Front of Pitshanger Manor, 1801

Martinware fireplace, 1891 (made for Billiards Room, Buscot Park, Oxon.)

hanced by using the well-illustrated (and modestly-priced) guidebook. The great achievement of the restoration work at Pitshanger Manor has been the sheer attention to detail, ensuring that interiors have been restored in as authentic a way as possible, to return to rooms that Soane himself would have recognised and admired. A considerable amount of painstaking research went into taking paint scrapes to determine original colour schemes, and into studying drawings and documents for the house in the Soane Museum, in order to come to scholarly conclusions about Soane's decorative intentions. This meticulous process was complicated by the changes that have obviously taken place since Soane's day in the design of some rooms.

A visit to Pitshanger Manor today enables a comparison to be made between those rooms built by George Dance, and Soane's interiors. Dance was responsible for the Eating Room, and the Drawing Room above it. The Eating Room has been decorated in colours close to the original paint scheme, and an Edwardian extension is regularly used for the museum's lively programme of temporary exhibitions. The Drawing Room (on the first floor)

contains items of furniture on loan from the Hull-Grundy bequest, though in Soane's day it was used to display what he described as 'many works by modern masters, a large collection of books, manuscripts and drawings relating to the Fine Arts and particularly to Architecture.' The restoration of this room shows the care that went into the project. Paint samples were taken, which showed that the colour scheme corresponded to that in watercolour sketches of the room made by one of Soane's own pupils in 1832 (illustrated in the guidebook). These sketches were followed in the resplendent and elaborate Chinese wallpaper used in the restoration.

The grand scale of the Eating Room is ample preparation for the more intimate, but still breathtaking beauties of the Library and Breakfast Room, which adjoin each other on the ground floor. The original decorative scheme for the Library was known from a large collection of preparatory drawings in the Soane Museum, and most of this

scheme has been superbly recreated, with particular attention to the cross-vaulted ceiling. The Breakfast Room, however, is the triumph of the house, with its lavish marbling, bronzing, and porphyry finishes, leading to the ceiling, with its clouds in a bright blue sky.

The Library leads to a gallery – the Martinware Room – where a major collection of Martinware pottery from the Hull-Grundy bequest is displayed in sympathetic, late-Victorian-style surroundings. The centrepiece of the room is a massive and unique fireplace made in 1891 for Alexander Henderson's house in Oxfordshire, and eventually gifted by a descendant to Southall and Norwood Urban District Council, now part of the London Borough of Ealing. The collection of pots on display is a good and representative one, showing both functional wares, such as jugs and vases, and the more eccentric bird jars and miniature pieces. The museum guidebook has a good summary of the work of the Martin brothers, and their ceramic output.

The Library, Pitshanger Manor, 1986 (redecoration based on original colour scheme)

Pollock's Toy Museum

1 Scala Street, London W1P 1LJ
01-636 3452
⊖ Goodge Street ⇌ Euston,
Kings Cross
Closed Sundays. 🚻 ♿ SG
🚹 & 🚺 book in advance by phone;
maximum 30 people.

A visit to the Pollock's Toy Museum is always a success. Here in the centre of town, housed in two small, interconnecting Georgian houses, resides one of the most charming, crowded, and enchanting small museums in London. A bright and energetically-painted frieze on the exterior walls of the house catches the eye of any passer-by, and prepares the visitor for a crammed and cramped visual feast. The entrance to the museum is through Pollock's Theatrical Print Warehouse (where toy theatres are sold), and the modest entrance charge to the museum is cashed in by an impressive cast-metal till.

The museum visit is certainly an adventure in itself, as the access to each tiny room is through narrow entrances and up steep steps. Yet the journey to the top of the museum and

London bus by Wells-Brimtoy Ltd, c. 1936

Exterior, Pollocks Toy Museum

down again through the very well-stocked shop is worth the physical effort. Exploring the museum is like entering a secret world of play, in a strange private house crammed with cases and objects. The whole mood of the building is friendly, and somehow out of keeping with the times. It couldn't be a more appropriate building to engage and entertain the visitor, even though it is probably wisest to plan a visit out of school holiday periods and weekends.

The character of the Toy Museum is captured by many historically-important objects, including Eric, 'the oldest-known teddy bear'. Eric looks worse for wear now, but defiantly happy amongst his fellow bears, many dating from before 1910. The museum collection is very varied, comprising good examples of optical toys, space toys, early jigsaws, puppets, dolls, games, and toy theatres. Toys from Britain and all around the world belong in this comprehensive collection, which has examples from the 18th century to the present day.

The museum is named after Benjamin Pollock (1856–1937), who ran a

Cover of children's magazine, 1898

shop in East London that acquired a reputation for manufacturing toy theatres. Pollock took over his father-in-law's business at a time when toy

British Tommy, *First World War army doll, 1916*

theatres were a well-established part of domestic entertainment. He ran the business, producing lithographs of toy theatres, for 60 years. Pollock's shop in Hoxton, in the east end of London, was one of the very last stockists and creators of toy theatres; trade fell in the late 19th century due to competition from other forms of entertainment, such as the 'penny dreadful' magazines of the 1860s and '70s. Mr Pollock's shop became fashionable again in the 1920s, when famous stage actors such as Ellen Terry and Charlie Chaplin visited Hoxton. The tradition of toy theatre was kept alive after Pollock's death by an antiquarian bookseller. Finally, more or less by chance, the stock of toy theatres came into the possession of new owners – Pollocks Toy Theatres Ltd. The establishment of the museum in the 1950s (on another site) was undertaken as a publicity exercise for the business. It has since developed and grown, with its own momentum, into the varied and important collection of today. Regular temporary exhibitions are held here, and the museum is a much-cherished venue for children and adults alike.

Ranger's House

Chesterfield Walk, Blackheath, London SE10   01-853 0035
⊖ New Cross (some distance)
⇌ Blackheath, Greenwich
Closes 4pm from 1 Oct to Maundy Thursday. 🆑 🅿
⟐ **A**: top floor inaccessible by wheelchair.
🚻 & 👫 contact: The Curator, The Iveagh Bequest, Kenwood, Hampstead Lane, London NW3 3JR (01 348 1286/7)

In a small upstairs room at the back of Ranger's House, there was at the time of my visit a graceful early-18th-century fan on display (on loan from the Greenwich Local History Library), which showed a peaceful and long-since changed view from One Tree Hill across Greenwich Park, over the Thames and beyond. Now that view contains (in addition to St Paul's Cathedral) the slender, lean pinnacles of the Barbican Estate's tower blocks, and the flurry of new Docklands building along the banks of the River. In 1730, so the anonymous painter of the fan would have us believe, a procession of windmills round a meander in the Thames acted as a backdrop for a party of aristocratic walkers. The fan was highly appropriate in this setting, not

Exterior, Ranger's House

only for the historic perspective it brought to today's view across the royal parklands, but also because of the hint it gave of another major historic building project in the centre of Greenwich, the new *Fan Museum*. Greenwich has always given good value to London's cultural visitor (there are very important attractions, such as the **National Maritime Museum** and the **Cutty Sark**, nearby) yet Ranger's House, perhaps because of its slightly distant position from the centre of the village, is often left out of the visitor's itinerary.

There are many good reasons, however, for a visit to the House. Sitting in the galleries on a summer's evening listening to music or poetry (from the regular programme of concerts), is a civilised occupation, especially as the pleasure is increased by the prospect of looking at a very important collection of paintings, and, appropriately enough, musical instruments.

Since 1974, Ranger's House has been home to the Suffolk Collection of paintings – a generous gift made to the Greater London Council, specifically for the House, by the son and daughter-in-law of the 19th Earl of Suffolk and Berkshire. At the heart of this collection is a magnificent series of full-length Jacobean portraits by William Larkin, displayed to very good effect in the Long Gallery added to the House in the mid 18th century. Of particular note are Larkin's rich, formal, and highly accurate female portraits, which may have been painted for the marriage of Thomas Howard to Elizabeth Cecil in 1614, and are known as the 'Berkshire Marriage Set'. The portraits give an idea of the sumptuous nature of aristocratic and courtly life in 17th century England, and there is an arrogant pride to the poses that must have pleased the sitters. Larkin's earlier painting of Richard Sackville, for example, shows the third Earl of Dorset with a beady stare, one hand impatiently resting on his hip, and wearing a very extravagant pair of ornate shoes topped with huge rosettes (colour plate 23). He was known as 'a man of spirit and talent', as well as 'a licentious spendthrift', and perhaps in

William Larkin, Lady Dorothy Cary, *c. 1615 (detail)*

his penetrating stare at the painter we may recognise how well Larkin has caught the complexity and opposing sides of his sitter's character.

The Suffolk Collection also contains other notable 17th century portraits by artists such as Cornelius Johnson and Kneller, all displayed to advantage in the unassuming and peaceful rooms of the House.

The period first floor rooms of Ranger's House are now used to display musical instruments from the Dolmetsch Collection, on loan from the **Horniman Museum**. Familiar instruments, such as oboes, harpsichords and guitars, are shown with early instruments from Arnold Dolmetsch's collection – the archlute, hurdy-gurdy, and viol. An appealing touch in an otherwise rather formal display is the use of open music scores at some of the harpsichords, as if the instruments were just about to be played.

An inexpensive fold-out colour pamphlet on the instruments describes the pioneering work of Arnold Dolmetsch (1858–1940), who used his post of violin teacher at Dulwich College to educate students about the principles of early music, rather than imposing dreary repetition of exercises for their own sake. Dolmetsch was a collector and a craftsman, and the instruments on display include the meti-

culously painted Green Harpsichord of 1896, which was his first harpsichord and made at William Morris's suggestion. But his collection of instruments is also international, and features elaborate Portuguese guitars and Italian archlutes.

As the instruments must rest mute in their exhibition cases, the visitor may admire them for their sometimes strange shapes or elaborate carving; it is good, in a way, to view the collection as 'furniture', since there are numerous items of period furniture displayed around Ranger's House. Regular visitors will no doubt keep a careful eye on the restoration project taking place in the bedroom on the first floor, where an early-18th-century four-poster Angel bed will be transformed through the addition of suitable and historically accurate hangings.

The final pleasure of visiting Ranger's House is in the building itself, a symmetrical red-brick villa built probably around 1705 for Admiral Hosier on the 'Waste' at the edge of Greenwich Park, overlooking Blackheath. The House was later the home of the Earl of Chesterfield (the author of the famous *Letters* to his son) and of the Duchess of Brunswick (mother of Queen Caroline); in 1815 it became the official residence of the Ranger of Greenwich Park.

The Green Harpsichord by Arnold Dolmetsch with painted decoration by Helen Coombe, 1896

Royal Air Force Museum

Hendon, London NW9 5LL
01-205 2266
⊖ Colindale ⇌ Mill Hill Broadway
Open daily. 🚻 🖼 ℗ ♿ WG
🚻 discount: information from Marketing Department (01 200 1763). 👫 annual ticket for schools, details and application form from Education Officer (ext. 215/229).

The improbable combination of a huge Blackburn Beverley C I Transport aircraft and an RAF launch, sitting in the middle of the museum's car park, make a spectacular, and slightly surreal, introduction to this major complex of buildings.

The site has had a history of flying exploits since Claude Grahame-White became fascinated by the achievements of the Wright Brothers and Louis Bleriot, who made the first powered crossing of the English Channel by air in 1909. Grahame-White established a centre for aviation enthusiasts at Hendon, alongside his aircraft factory, which was commandeered for military aviation early in the First World War. It is particularly fitting that the story of air warfare is told here today by one of the world's most important collections of historic aircraft.

The first impression inside the Royal Air Force Museum's Aircraft Hall will be one of sheer amazement at

Vulcan B2

Bristol F.2B fighters

the size of the great hangars, and the serried ranks of brightly-polished aircraft and vehicles. It is possible to get face to face here with some of the best-known World War II aircraft. The Supermarine Spitfire I is perhaps the most famous fighter aircraft in history (and certainly the airplane beside which visitors most want their photograph taken). Its heavy armament and sleek lines compare with the frail and horrifyingly exposed early machines like the Bleriot XI, which was used as a training aircraft for the Royal Flying Corps during the First World War.

The mixed arrangement of exhibits in the Aircraft Hall makes a comparison between aircraft of different generations easy, and the panoramic view across the vast space adds to the hangar-like atmosphere. The display includes Second World War aircraft, together with other European and early jet aircraft. The British Aircraft Corporation (English Electric) Lightning holds an important place as the first truly supersonic aircraft to be used by the RAF, which will probably be the last British single-seat fighter to be built. The example shown is the F6, the final operational type.

The Aircraft Hall tells the story of aviation history by concentrating solely on the aircraft themselves. Around the Hall are galleries that give the human detail behind the aircraft, and concentrate on personalities or themes, such as training. The Art Gallery shows paintings from the museum's large collection, including works by well known artists such as Elizabeth Frink, Laura Knight, Graham Sutherland, and

Michael Ayrton. The displays are regularly changed, and temporary exhibitions are held here too. A permanent exhibition of War Artists' work is displayed in the Dermot Boyle Wing. The exhibitions play an important role in the museum's work: through looking at paintings it is often easier to get a sense beyond the great machinery and aircraft on display to the actual sensation of flying. They bring alive, for example, all the noise, discomfort, exhilaration, and terror that must have accompanied flying on a night bombing raid.

Other memorable galleries include Gallery 2, which shows a Royal Flying Corps and Royal Naval Air Service workshop, complete with engines, tools

and aircraft. The formal memorabilia of service life are shown through displays of medals, orders, and decorations given to senior servicemen, including Lord Trenchard (the first Chief of the Air Staff), and Winston Churchill, who held the honorary rank of Air Commodore.

On June 8th, 1940, Churchill gave a famous speech to the House of Commons, broadcast across Britain. He concluded: 'What General Weygand called the Battle of France is over. I expect that the Battle of Britain is about to begin.' German tactics were to send over armadas of bombers to render the Royal Air Force incapable of opposing the following seaborne invasion force. The great air battle that ensued during the summer months of 1940 became known as the Battle of Britain, and it is this historic moment of aerial warfare that is recorded in the outstanding Battle of Britain Hall, a separate building in the RAF Museum complex.

Through the display of British, German, and Italian aircraft, with very effective supporting dioramas, the Battle of Britain Hall gives a vivid insight into the experience and sensations of life during the 1940s. The crucial role of the Womens Voluntary Service in

Aircrew waiting in readiness to 'scramble', Second World War

wartime London is described, for example, and the chilling sound of airplanes and wail of air raid sirens adds a realistic dimension to the aircraft display.

There are famous aircraft here in abundance, from the Hawker Hurricane (the first of the RAF's eight-gun monoplane fighters), which played a lethally destructive part in the Battle of Britain, to the Heinkel HeIII, the best known of the Luftwaffe's bombers, displayed here in its factory colour scheme. The administrative work of coordinating Britain's defence during the Battle is shown through a reconstruction of the Group Operations Room at RAF Uxbridge, set out as it was at 11.30 am on 15th September, 1940, remembered as 'Battle of Britain Day'.

The third major element of the museum complex is the Bomber Command Hall, opened in 1983. At the entrance of the huge gallery is the awesome sight of 'S for Sugar', the most famous of all Avro Lancaster Bombers, the aircraft type renowned for the attack in the Second World War on the Möhne and Eder dams. 'S for Sugar' flew over 137 bombing sorties. The huge frames and wings of the aircraft on display in the Bomber Command Hall are thrown into perspective by the almost miniature appearance of the cars and bomb trolleys that they dwarf. Walking under the dark and forbidding delta wing of the Avro Vulcan is an almost menacing experience, and reminds one of the use of the aircraft in contemporary conflict during the Falklands War.

The most extraordinary aircraft on display here is the hulk of a Handley Page Halifax Bomber, recovered from Lake Hoklingen in Norway, and the sole surviving example of its type. The museum's decision not to restore it to factory condition (thereby creating, in effect, a replica) is intended as a tribute to a great bomber, and it reveals by comparison the quality of restoration work on the rest of the museum's unique and highly important collection of aircraft. This is a memorable museum of aviation history, and of the history of aerial warfare.

Royal Armouries

HM Tower of London, London
EC3N 4AB   01-480 6358
⊖ Tower Hill ⇌ Fenchurch Street, Cannon Street , London Bridge
Closed on Sunday mornings throughout the year, and on Sunday afternoons from Nov. to Feb. 🖫 to the Tower of London.
& S: phone in advance and warders will give assistance.
🖫 & 🖫 must book in writing at least 2 weeks in advance: contact Receiver of Fees Office (01 709 0765 ext. 235);
pre-booked 🖫 ▣ September–April. Education programmes and materials by prior arrangement with Education Centre (01 480 6358 ext. 332).

The Royal Armouries, at the Tower of London, has the distinction of being Britain's oldest national museum, as well as the country's first public museum. The Tower of London stretches over a 16 acre site, consisting of a classic example of a medieval concentric castle, developed from an early Norman banked enclosure within the south-east corner of the Roman city walls. It was built on the orders of William the Conqueror, as part of his policy for consolidating the authority he had gained by victory at the Battle of Hastings and his coronation on Christmas Day, 1066. The building of the White Tower, the earliest stone fortification at the Tower of London, commenced in 1078. It took twenty years to build, using Londoners' forced labour, with massive walls of Kentish ragstone faced with limestone. The White Tower was regularly whitewashed, hence its name.

The Royal Armouries is the premier collection of arms and armour in the country. The Tower is also home to the *Herald's Museum* and the *Museum of the Royal Fusiliers*. The majority of the Armouries collection is exhibited in the White Tower, continuing a tradition of displaying armour that dates back to at least the 16th century. It is also still possible to see signs of habitation inside the Tower, such as fireplaces and garderobes (lavatories), and the remarkable Chapel of St John, a beautiful and early example of Norman church architecture. The Chapel

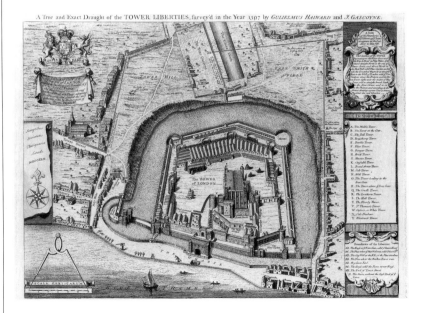

Engraving of the Tower of London, 1597

would originally have been highly decorated with wall paintings, but was stripped during the Reformation.

The need for more comfortable Royal surroundings led to the development of the Royal Palace here under the reign of Henry III. Of this complex only the Wakefield Tower survives: one room has been restored using detailed contemporary descriptions. At this time, too, an inner ward was built – a defensive wall that can be walked along via the 'wall walk'. In the reign of Henry's son, Edward I, the outer wall was built. Entry to the Royal Palace could only be gained by passing through a number of towers, drawbridges, and portcullises. The first of these was the Lion Tower, now the site of a gift shop outside the main entrance; it used to house the Royal Menagerie. Henry III kept an elephant at the Tower, and other animals included lions, leopards, and even a polar bear. The animals left the Tower to become part of the new London zoo early in the 19th century.

Visitors to the Tower of London can tour a number of the Towers in the inner ward, including the Beauchamp Tower, with inscriptions by some of its famous prisoners, such as Robert Dudley, later Earl of Leicester and Elizabeth I's favourite, and his brother, Guildford, husband of Lady Jane Grey. Sir Walter Raleigh was imprisoned, albeit in fairly comfortable surroundings, in the Bloody Tower. Life was more spartan in the Salt Tower, where Catholic priests were imprisoned. The Royal Armouries' collection of instruments of torture and punish-

Armour for man and horse, late 15th century

Grotesque helmet, early 16th century

ment is displayed in the Bowyer Tower, including the block and axe used at the last public execution on Tower Hill in 1747.

In the White Tower are the main displays from the Armouries, including weapons from Saxon and Norman times, up to the English Civil War. There are mail shirts and weapons like those seen in the Bayeaux Tapestry, as well as full-plate armour developed later to repel more efficient arrows and swords. This progression culminated in the impressive armours of Henry VIII, who was highly skilled in foot and horse combat. His great suits of armour made in the Royal workshops at Greenwich are displayed here, as well as a grotesque helmet made for the King by the court armourer of Maximilian I.

Armour eventually gave way to new forms of battledress when guns were introduced, against which plate armour stood little chance. The Royal Armouries includes an impressive collection of early muskets and sporting weaponry – even whaling harpoons. In the New Armouries is displayed the British Military Armoury, with examples of practically every weapon ever made and designed at the Tower, from the time of the Civil Wars to the Crimean War. Displays include the development of the bayonet, and – in common with other labelling throughout the Armouries – are strangely unrelated to the actual physical effects of these instruments of war. Above this is the 18th and 19th Century Armoury, which includes a display of machine-guns (first developed during the American Civil War, 1861–65), laid out in front of a sepia frieze of a war-torn landscape.

The Waterloo Barracks (begun in 1845 after a great fire in a storehouse in 1841) contains displays of Oriental Armoury, including some dramatic Japanese armour, and the imposing Indian elephant armour brought to England by Lord Clive and said to have been captured in his victory at Plassey in 1757.

From the time of Henry VIII onwards, the Tower was used less as the home of Kings and Queens – Hampton Court and Whitehall were more popular – but it retained its other roles as a royal palace: it was a prison, whence people such as Sir Walter Raleigh and Sir Thomas More were sent for execution; it was also a mint, a repository for the Crown Jewels, and above all the greatest arsenal of the Kingdom. The Crown Jewels have been shown in Waterloo Barracks since 1967. They include the Crown of St Edward, used at coronations, the Imperial State Crown and the Sceptre, with the Cross containing the Star of Africa, the largest cut diamond in the world. This exhibition is nearly always very busy, and it is worth bearing in mind that you have to carry on walking around the Crown Jewels on the first level, or stop and look on the second upper hall.

The Yeomen Warders (*not* Beefeaters!) were given the right to wear their royal livery in Edward VI's reign. They give guided tours to the Tower of London that last about an hour, and, with their anecdotes and tall stories, are tailor-made for tourists.

Science Museum

Exhibition Road, London SW7 2DD
01-938 8000
⊖ South Kensington
Closed Sunday mornings. 🚻 ▣
♿ **WG**: special lifts, please contact uniformed staff for assistance.
🎫 & 👥 must book in advance in writing, through Education Department (01 938 8222).

The huge cathedral-like main hall of the Science Museum is an awesome place to start a museum visit. Recently renovated, with huge-scale slides of objects from the collection depicted on hi-tech banners, the museum spectacle is visually remarkable. As with the other great national museums at South Kensington, there is far too much to take in comfortably during a single visit. Even just one or two of the principal galleries will contain a substantial amount of information and exhibits, and it would be wise to make a careful selection before embarking, along with many thousands of other visitors, on the museum trip.

When Prince Albert suggested, after the runaway success of the Great Exhibition in 1851, that its profits should be used to buy land south of Kensington Gore for institutions that would advance the 'industrial pursuits of all nations', he instigated a great museum plan. The Science and the Victoria and Albert Museums – on opposite sides of Exhibition Road – grew from this royal vision. It took until 1909 to separate formally the two museums and their

The locomotive, Caerphilly Castle

respective arts and science collections, and much building work throughout the 20th century for the Science Museum to house the growing, substantial – and in the case of some objects, huge – material evidence of human progress in science and industry. The creation of the National Railway Museum at York, and the National Museum of Photography, Film and Television at Bradford (likewise part of the National Museum of Science and Industry), demonstrates the growing influence of this national museum.

The Science Museum has always been one of the most popular of Britain's national museums. The collections are arranged in logical sequences – from the introductory gallery looking out over the East Hall, to sections on everything from Domestic Appliances to Marine Engineering, Optics to Iron and Steel, and Plastics to Astronomy. The free museum plan has a clear diagram showing galleries and their floor levels.

There are spectacular sights and surprises everywhere. Displayed as part of the comprehensive and minutely-detailed ship-model collection, for example, is a model of a very unstately-looking water velocipede built for Queen Victoria. There are objects that are very familiar to the nation's scientific consciousness, such

Worm's-eye view of a satellite launcher

Full-scale section of an Advanced Gas-cooled Reactor core

as Stephenson's 'Rocket' of 1829. Others appeal simply because of their proximity: standing beside 'Black Arrow', Britain's own satellite launch vehicle (in the good, cheerful, modern gallery, 'The Exploration of Space') makes what would ordinarily have been an impossible proximity, a fine and commonplace event. It's a feeling common, too, in the Transport Gallery, which has a suitably garage-like appearance. Although it is one of the museum's less forgiving displays, with a didactic mood to many of the museum labels, it is still popular with inquisitive visitors. The sheer size of objects such as the 1923 Great Western Railway locomotive, 'Caerphilly Castle', will always be impressive. It is matched for grandeur today by the sight of the massive 1903 Mill Engine from Burnley Ironworks in action: stately, clean and bright, it is a symbol of the powerful progress of the Industrial Revolution. Paintings in the museum's collection like Philip de Loutherbourg's 'Coalbrookdale by

Night' give a more dramatic pictorial expression of the devastating effects on the quality of human life made possible by such awesome machines.

The exhibition, 'Clothes for the Job', on the third floor takes an interesting perspective on industrial life. The museum's collection contains a rich group of special clothes used in industry, sport, and domestic situations. On display there are examples of bullet-resistant garments, space-suits and other flying clothing, cricket-wear, and the total protection afforded by an ice-hockey goal-minder's attire.

One of the most eagerly-visited parts of the museum is 'Launch Pad', which has opened and run to wide acclaim. It represents the museum's attempts to involve its young visitors in the art of scientific discovery, rather than presenting scientific opinion through the safety and anonymity of information labels. 'Launch Pad' gives visitors the chance to carry out experiments and demonstrations, to explore aspects of technology and engineering. It always

15th century Astrolabe

provokes enthusiasm and keen interest.

So, too, though in a less interactive way, will the Wellcome Museum of the History of Medicine, one of the most outstanding galleries in the whole of the Science Museum. It sets out to demonstrate the development of medical knowledge through very effective models and reconstructed surgeries, and the display of a superb collection. The experience is at times grim: dioramas showing military surgery in the 16th century, and Naval Surgery in 1800, are almost painful to look at, so graphic and detailed are they. It's a gallery that makes the concept of a national public health service seem even more profoundly necessary to a civilised society.

From the colourful and atmospheric display of holograms in the Optics Gallery, to the surprising sight of aircraft hung ambitiously from the ceiling of the Aeronautics Gallery, the Science Museum achieves its main objective of bringing entertainment to learning about the scientific and industrial heritage of the world. It is a museum that is (as it must be) at the forefront of scientific knowledge, and a place where the use of today's technology, such as the use of video disc (in 'The Domesday Project') and satellite broadcasting, can be taken for granted.

Sir John Soane's Museum

13 Lincoln's Inn Fields, London
WC2A 3BP   01-405 2107
⊖ Holborn
Closed Sundays and Mondays. **F**
♿ **S**: no lift to upper floors.
⊞ & **⋈** must book in advance.

The great architect, Sir John Soane (1753–1837), has probably had more influence on the modern museum world in London than any other single person, given that **Dulwich Picture Gallery** (designed by Soane), **Pitshanger Manor** (part rebuilt and lived in by Soane), and the Bank of England (Soane's best-known work, and home of the *Bank of England Museum*) are open to the public.

Soane's own museum, at 13 Lincoln's Inn Fields, was his home for the last 24 years of his life. He also designed the two adjacent houses, making a grand and well-ordered architectural composition facing the Fields. The Museum is a delight from the moment one enters, and is greeted by the helpful and courteous atten-

dants. The situation, the collection, and the sheer idiosyncracy of the museum make it one of the most enjoyable places to visit and revisit in the centre of London. The building has the feel of a loved and cherished home, in spite of the academic nature of many of the collections.

The house is crammed literally floor to ceiling with works of art and antiquities collected by Soane for display in his house, which became a living museum of one person's taste. Old-fashioned explanatory labels assist today's visitor in understanding more about individual rooms and objects, and there is a detailed (if rather formal) guide, *A New Description of Sir John Soane's Museum* for those seeking further information.

It is, however, the atmosphere of the house rather than any single object that remains longest in the memory – the feeling of a great clutter of culture, and of rooms densely packed with sculpture, paintings, vases, models, and furniture.

Soane determined some five years before his death to establish his house and collection as a museum, to be enjoyed by all in perpetuity, and he

William Hogarth, A Rake's Progress, The Heir, *1733–34*

secured a private Act of Parliament to achieve this public-spirited end. The Bill was introduced in the House of Commons by the radical politician, Joseph Hume, and makes plain Soane's wish that the House and Museum should be left 'as nearly as possible in the style in which Sir John Soane shall leave it'. The house and collection were therefore created with a singular unity of purpose, and a forceful antiquarian vision. There are domestic triumphs (such as the sumptuous rich yellow of the South Drawing Room), and rather whimsical touches: the Breakfast Parlour presents 'a series of those fanciful effects, which constitute the poetry of architecture', and all over the house there are mirrors to reflect the great collections back to the visitors' astonished gaze. The collections are testament to Soane's wide-ranging tastes, and to the great wealth that enabled him to indulge them by steady addition. He bought the best examples from many civilisations – Egypt, Greece, Rome – as well as commissioning contemporary works of art.

Among the most extraordinary rooms in the house is the Monk's Parlour, which Soane added in 1824 (at the same time as his Picture Room), created as a Gothic fantasy for the imaginary Padre Giovanni. The room contains a number of casts from medieval buildings, some stained glass, and wood carvings, and has a view through a window to the Monk's Yard, containing mock ruins of the Monk's Cloister (built of fragments from the old House of Lords and Westminster Hall). The feel of this part of the house is grotesque and gloomy – partly an ironic comment by Soane on the fashionable cult of antiquarianism, but perhaps also a reflection of a more sombre frame of mind, as Soane's mood after the deaths of his wife and son was more reclusive. The Sepulchral Chamber is also gloomily named, yet it contains one of the greatest objects from Soane's collection, the sarcophagus of Seti I. This was discovered in 1817 in the tomb chamber of Seti I (1303–1290 BC) in the Valley of the Kings, and was first offered to the

Exterior view, 13 Lincoln's Inn Fields

British Museum, who turned it down on grounds of expense.

The Dome is the oldest part of the museum, and Soane used it to dramatic effect to display a crowded collection of antiquities (colour plate 7). Casts and original sculptures are crammed into the small space, surveyed, appropriately enough, by Sir Francis Chantrey's marble bust of Soane, presented in 1830.

The Picture Room on the ground floor is a small room specifically designed to show the maximum number of pictures: paintings are displayed (characteristically for this period) to ceiling height, as well as on a series of hinged panels. The great sets of paintings by William Hogarth, 'A Rake's

Progress' and 'An Election', are displayed here, along with works by Watteau and Piranesi, and a good selection of Soane's own architectural drawings (including the interior rooms of Pitshanger Manor and the Bank of England).

The Dining Room gives an inkling of the informed and academic conversations that must have been a regular feature of life in the house. Yet the museum today maintains an approachable and even friendly air, because it is so completely authentic: every object tells a story about Soane's own taste and character. If time is short, then a visit to this museum alone will be bound to create a lasting and happy impression.

Tate Gallery

Millbank, London SW1P 4RG
01-821 1313
Recorded information 01-821 7128
⊖ Pimlico ⇌ Vauxhall
Closed Sunday mornings. ☐ but
charge for major loan exhibitions. ▣
⟁ W: wheelchairs available, limited
number allowed in building at any
one time; use Atterbury Street
entrance, advance warning
required; ramp and lift access to
main floor.
⛉ & ⛉ book with Education
Department at least four weeks in
advance (ext. 343). ☺

The early history of the Tate Gallery
tells an all-too-familiar story of pressure brought to hear on an unwilling (if
not actually philistine) British government of the 19th century. Plans to
establish a national gallery of modern
British art were advanced by the collector, Henry Tate. He had amassed a
fortune through his sugar empire (with
plantations run by slave labour), and
made the visionary and philanthropic
gesture to build the nation such a
gallery on condition that the government provided a suitable site. Eventually the site occupied by London's
largest prison was chosen, and from an
all-too-typical beginning of prevarica-
tion by the state, a great, national art
gallery was founded at Millbank on the
Thames.

The Tate Gallery was purpose-built
in a neo-classical style and opened to
the public in 1897. It houses the nation's collection of British paintings, or
more precisely historic British paintings (from the European Renaissance
in the early 16th century to the beginning of modern art at the end of the
19th century), and Modern painting
(which incudes both British and foreign painting and sculpture). The gallery spaces suit this historical division,
and are arranged in a chronological
way, with historic British paintings to
the left of the lobby area, and Modern
Art and the Turner Bequest to the
right. There are frequent changes to
the display, and a regular and ambi-

Barry Flanagan, a nose in repose, *1977–79*

tious programme of educational events,
and temporary exhibitions.

The idea of modern art has always
courted dismissive, and even aggres-
sive publicity, and the Tate has been
no stranger to complaints about elitism
and irrelevance. The furore that
greeted the gallery's purchase of Carl
Andre's infamous 'Bricks' gave rise to
some particularly noisy comments from
the reactionary press. And yet the di-

verse, enthusiastic and knowledgeable
audience that makes the Tate such a
busy and crowded gallery seems to
make a clear point about the popularity
of modern art.

The chronological sequence of galleries provides a helpful perspective for
the visitor. A tour will often start with
the formal and rather stiff 17th century
paintings of members of the aristocra-
cy. There are livelier works to follow,

notably the flowing and graceful portrait of the Italian dancer, Giovanna Baccelli, by Gainsborough (colour plate 1). There are important groups of works here by many of the major British artists, such as Reynolds, Constable, Blake, Hogarth, and the Pre-Raphaelites. The British sporting artist, George Stubbs, is represented by famous paintings like the 'Horse frightened by a Lion', and by other quieter, rural scenes. There is an impressive sequence of John Martin's remarkable apocalyptic paintings. In the rooms devoted to the Modern collection, the whole mood and architecture of the gallery changes. Gone is the slightly scholarly air of the historic rooms. The restrained and cool, white backdrop to the modern paintings is highly effective, and throughout the galleries there is a sympathetic display of many items from the sculpture collection. Great works from

Samuel Palmer, The Harvest Moon, *1831–32*

Claes Oldenburg, Lipsticks in Piccadilly Circus, *1966*

the Impressionist period onwards are shown here, as well as compelling paintings by Picasso, Dali, and Braque. Works by Ben Nicholson, Barbara

David Hockney, My Parents, *1977*

Edward Burra, The Snack Bar, *1930*

Hepworth, and Henry Moore emphasise the major British contribution to
modern art. Peter Blake, David Hockney, and Ceri Richards are among
those whose works are included in the
comprehensive national collection of
20th century British Art.

The great Turner Bequest to the
nation was finally honoured by a new
purpose-built gallery designed by
James Stirling and opened in 1987, the
Clore Gallery. This handsome extension, with some bright details on the
exterior walls, does the artist's bequest
justice. The arrangement of paintings
is helpful, the information labels worth
studying, and the grand sweep of Turner's art is presented most effectively.
The clumsy portraits, as well as the
magisterial late landscapes, are all
here. There is also a display case full of
Turner's work tools – the paint thin-
ners, boxes, palettes, and studio pig-
ment cabinet – and a room devoted to
his watercolours.

The Tate Gallery has ambitious development proposals to carry on the
spectacular achievements made in the
late 1980s. The Tate Gallery Liverpool has recently opened, and major
projects include a Sculpture Museum,
a Museum of New Art, and a Museum
and a Study Centre of 20th century
Art, all on the Millbank site.

Telecom Technology Showcase

*135 Queen Victoria Street, London
EC4V 4AT   01-248 7444*
Free information 0800 289689
⊖ Blackfriars, St Paul's
⇌ Blackfriars
Closed Saturdays and Sundays. ☐
♿ X: prior notice of visit desirable.
♿ & ♿ must book in advance.
Educational videos available by
prior arrangement.

Telecom Technology Showcase is one
of a new breed of museums. It is
designed to very high standards, has a
colourful 'hi-tech' appearance, and is
full of interactive exhibits exhorting the
visitor to switch on a video or fax a
message. It is usually full, too, of visitors obviously impressed by the quality
of the museum. 'Britain's Museum of
Telecommunications' sets out to tell a
story of how people communicate with
each other. It deals with the complex-
ities behind this seemingly straightforward message with style, purpose, and
the occasional touch of humour.

THE SPEAKING CLOCK

If you want the correct time at any hour during the day
or night, you can get in touch with the Post Office
Speaking Clock, in a few moments, by telephone.
The Speaking Clock is an electro-mechanical device
which announces the time correct to one-tenth of a
second at ten-second intervals.
Simply ring up your exchange and ask for
The Speaking Clock.
The charge for the service is the same as for a call
to Central London.

Publicity for the Speaking Clock service

The history of the telecommunications industry is one of rapid advances
and major technological discoveries.
The pace of change in today's information technology is astounding, and the
Showcase makes it seem even more so
by putting the story in historical context. The modest scale of the museum,
and the clearly worded and well laid
out exhibits, make the connections between the first and pioneering discoveries in electromagnetics, and the
advances of optical fibre technology,
easy to understand. There's a good
deal of information on offer here, but it
is presented in a modern, visually-
attractive style, with careful use of
many working exhibits.

There are some excellent touches.
Beside a display of several very modish
1930s telephones a video of a short
GPO film Unit musical, 'The Fairy of
the Phone', is well worth watching.
There are some well-made dioramas,
including a realistic trench warfare display with a soldier operating a crude
field telephone, and a particularly well-
presented interactive display on digital
transmission. The final video in the
Showcase, 'What Next', makes the
possibilities now open to the communications industry seem endless.

On the floor beside the Showcase
entrance ('Deck level'), the story of
telecommunication is told through a
sequence of exhibits looking at specific
historical themes or subjects, such as
'Early Telegraphs', 'Radio', 'The
1930s', and 'The Digital Revolution'.

Modern telecommunications started
with the telegraph. The earliest examples were developed in France in 1794
by Claude Chaffe, who pioneered a
visual semaphore system, relaying
messages along towers situated on hill-
tops up to ten miles apart. The poten-
tial of electricity to carry messages with
speed was soon realised, and Cooke
and Wheatstone invented the first
practical application, the electric Five
Needle Telegraph, in 1837. Cooke
advanced his work to make communications between railway stations –
to signal train movements – more reliable, and private telegraph companies
grew up to offer a public service. In
1868 the government sought to coun-

ter criticism of the private companies (which were notoriously unreliable and did not operate in unprofitable rural areas) by nationalising the industry, creating the Post Office as a government department. The Showcase illustrates, through early telegraph apparatus, the beginnings of what became a popular revolution in telecommunications. By 1885, we learn, 50 million telegrams a year were being sent on matters great and small; as Stanley Jevons remarked in 1876, 'Men have been known to telegraph for a clean pocket handkerchief.'

Workmen laying cement ducts for telephone cable, c. 1910

The development of the telephone is also shown, with a fine selection of elaborate early phones, and an explanation of the history behind the Post Office's move to take over the whole telephone system in Britain in 1912. There are some particularly good examples through the museum of the advertising material used by the Post Office to encourage the installation of phones; the 1930s design especially are highly regarded.

The role of telecommunications in the history of British life is effectively told at Showcase by concentrating on areas where communication has been particularly vital – during wartime or in public emergencies. The role of satellite communication is also revealed,

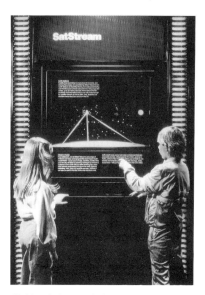

Children looking at the SatStream display

from the first launch of the 'early Bird' satellite in 1965 to the latest generation Intelsat V, which has a greatly enhanced capacity of voice circuits and television channels. The introduction of small dish aerials, which can receive signals from the new satellite systems, will give customers the opportunity to use a whole new range of services, such as television conferences, very rapid transfer of computer data, and cable television. The use of optical fibres to incease the capability of undersea cables will make transatlantic communications even more flexible.

Britain is living in an 'information society'. Telecom Technology Showcase reminds us of the historical perspective behind today's assumption that information is easy to get and quick to transmit. The physical task of creating our information systems is clearly laid out in the museum, particularly in the lower gallery, with its displays on the communications network, and the long sequence of pioneering discoveries by Marconi and Bell, which enable us to take communications for granted. It is a museum with an eye on the future, excellently supported by high-quality literature and outstandingly good displays.

Theatre Museum

1E Tavistock Street, London WC2E 7PA. Public entrance in Russell Street   01-836 7891 Recorded information 01-826 7624 Studio Theatre 01-836 2330
⊖ Covent Garden, Leicester Square, Charing Cross
⇌ Charing Cross
Closed Mondays. 🔲 📺 ♿ W G
🛗 contact General Manager two weeks in advance (01 836 5148).
♂♀ F by appointment.

The Theatre Museum was long expected, much delayed, and finally opened in subterranean galleries on the ground floor and basement of Covent Garden's Flower Market building. It is run as a branch of the **Victoria and Albert Museum**, and contains the finest collection of theatrical material in Britain.

The best place to begin a visit to the museum is in the classy and showy tearoom, where 'nothing is but what it seems'. Surrounded by a mural stage-set by Anthony Holland, complete with an hand-painted audience and interspersed with grand imitation marble pillars, this is a dramatic and colourful beginning to a museum visit. It is an

Hamlet *(Barrymore and Compton)*

Harry Hammond, Billie Holiday, *1959*

intriguing place to have theatrical conversations (talk carries here), or even to eavesdrop on those of the actors who seem to congregate here before their tour of the museum.

The tour begins with a dramatic descent down an inclined ramp with a colourul frieze of artists' handprints and signatures. The Main Gallery shows items from a huge and varied collection of objects to tell the story of the British stage and its development from Shakespearean drama to the present day. It draws upon a wide range of material, including paintings, watercolours, costumes, props, puppets, verbose playbills, dramatic posters, and intriguing model stage sets in a colourful evocation of theatrical history. Three major collections have been gathered together in the Theatre Museum, the principal one being Mrs Gabrielle Enthoven's wonderful mass of theatrical memorabilia, donated to the V & A in 1924. Additional collections built up by the Friends of the Museum of Performing Arts, and the British Theatre Museum Association, enrich the material on show.

There is a rather scholarly feel to the series of cases containing these mixed collections, which run along intimate corridors with plush walls. There are colourful touches: over the print of 'A View of the Fireworks and Illumina-

tions at His Grace the Duke of Richmond's on 15th May 1794', little coloured lights flash in the 'sky' in imitation of the original firework display. Each numbered case, or rather compartment, describes a theme or venue, such as 'Opera', or the 'Dressing Room'. In the formally-titled section, 'Light Entertainment: Rock & Pop',

there are some truly theatrical costumes, like Mick Jagger's 1972 jumpsuit – given, the label says in due deference, by Mick Jagger, Esq.

There are two atmospheric temporary exhibition galleries, named in honour of the great actors, Sir Henry Irving and Sir John Gielgud. One of the shows so far looked at the life and works of Gielgud; another was an excellent display (in a period setting) of the pop photographs of Harry Hammond, with resonant images of Nat King Cole on his first British Tour, or Buddy Holly during his only British Tour in 1958.

The Theatre Museum also contains a fascinating study collection displayed in the Harry R. Beard Room. It comprises Beard's reference collection of theatrical prints, drawings, paintings, and playbills, given by his brother and sister after his death in 1986. The collection, which is heavily used, is displayed rather uneasily in large pullout frames, and helpfully catalogued. There are some fetching touches, such as a proposed record sleeve for the first Sex Pistols record, 'Anarchy in the UK', and it is worth browsing for half an hour to come across historical gems

Robert Canning in Savage Earth, *from 'Dance – The World to Australia, Australia to the World'*

Mirror owned by the French actress, Réjane, and later by Peggy Ashcroft

Victoria and Albert Museum

*South Kensington, London SW7 2RL
01-938 8500   Recorded
information: 01-938 8441 (general),
01-938 8349 (exhibitions),
01-938 8638 (courses and events)*
⊖ South Kensington
Closed Sunday mornings. 🆅 ▣
♿ X G: wheelchairs available at
both entrances – contact Chief
Warder (01-938 8540); lifts to
upper floors, but some steps
between galleries; further
information 01-938 8362/5,
🚻 contact Education Service. ◉

In a case outside the smart new restaurant at the Victoria and Albert Museum there was at the time of my visit one of the strangest and most unforgettable objects in any museum collection – *Tippoo's Tiger*. It is a painted wooden figure of a tiger mauling a British soldier. Inside the tiger is a miniature organ that simulates the roars of the animal and the terrified groans of its victim. This macabre symbol of anti-imperialism was made for Tipu Sultan, the ruler of Mysore at the end of the 18th century, and was captured during the fall of Seringapatam when Tipu himself died. The Tiger was a popular exhibit in the East India Company's Museum in London, and is a highly popular exhibit at the V & A today.

In this one object are expressed feelings of rage, a political consciousness, and creativity and craft of a high enough standard to turn a cruel toy

like the urgent quotation in a 1976 Monstrous Regiment Company programme (in the section 'Drama: Feminist Theatre') from Jenny d'Hernicourt (1860): 'Woman is ripe for civic liberty, and we declare to you that . . . we shall regard as an enemy of progress and of the revolution anyone who comes out against our legitimate claim'.

To complete the visit to the Theatre Museum, the lower foyer, close to the Beard Room, is set up as a picture gallery, showing over a hundred theatrical paintings, mostly relating to performances on the London stage. Actors are shown in character, from David Garrick as Romeo in 1750, to Ian Holmes as Henry V in 1966. This gallery has the feel and colour of an Edwardian London theatre foyer, with its plush seats, marble pillars, large mirrors, and richly-coloured decoration. It is sometimes used for audiovisual presentations.

Chinese Apsara

into a work of art. Throughout the V & A a similar mix of talents has produced works of stunning beauty and interest in all fields of applied art and design. The V & A is the National Museum of Art and Design, and houses one of the world's greatest collections. Objects are of great diversity, and have come from all periods, and all cultures and countries – Europe, the Far East, South Asia, and the Islamic world. The collections include musical instruments, jewellery, furniture, metalwork, textiles and dress, paintings, photographs, ceramics and glass. This is also one of the largest museums in the world, with seven miles of galleries across a thirteen-acre site. So a visit is best given some forethought, and there are helpful maps and guides, together with an increasingly well-thought-out signposting system to orientate visitors once they have passed beyond the comforting sight of the entrance hall or information desk. The elegant museum guide suggests four complementary walks through the galleries – 'The Arts of the East', or 'British Art: Elizabeth I to Elizabeth II', for example – and describes in some detail the work of the museum's academic departments, and the nature of the museum's special collections (which include

The Canning Jewel, c. 1590

Tahitian Woman by Robert Gibbings

jewellery, the Raphael Cartoons, and the Dress Collection).

The V & A was founded as a result of the considerable (and profitable) success of the Great Exhibition of 1851, with the aim – which the museum still holds at the centre of its work – to encourage the highest standards of excellence among designers and manufacturers. The design of the museum itself reflects this proud and deliberately inspiring aim. Of particular note are the Morris, Gamble, and Poynter Rooms, the museum's original refreshment rooms, showing in turn William Morris's decorative designs (commissioned in 1866 by Henry Cole, the first director of the museum) in an Elizabethan Revival style, some colourful ceramic wall tiles and maiolica columns after designs by Gamble, and the original Dutch Kitchen and Grill Room, with Minton tiles painted by a class at the South Kensington Schools. These rooms, which have recently been restored, are a vivid reminder of the architectural heritage of the building. Changes in the V & A's interior landscape are happening with increased vigour as the museum looks to major corporate sponsors for redisplay of its fabulous collections. There are some distinctive and elegant achievements as a result of this policy: the discreet and understated Toshiba Gallery of Japanese Art, for example.

The cool symmetry of the new Medieval Treasury is very effective, and this gallery has some quite breathtaking objects, such as the Gloucester Candlestick, the only surviving work of early Norman art in metal, which rivals continental examples in grandeur and intricacy. Dragons and little men are entwined in the candlestick, which bears an inscription revealing that it was made for the Abbey of Gloucester under the rule of Abbot Peter (1104–13). The rich, glowing colours of medieval stained glass give a resonant backdrop to this fine gallery.

The delight of the Medieval Treasury, or the Jewellery Gallery, lies in its intimacy of scale. There is nothing low-key, however, about the Victorian Cast Court, with its momentous and towering collection of plaster casts taken from North European and Spanish art, and the huge cast of Trajan's column from Imperial Rome. In the 20th century galleries there are familiar and off-beat objects. It is difficult to

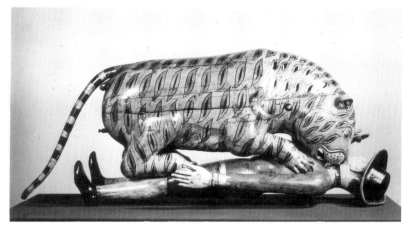
Tippoo's Tiger

Pot painted by Picasso, Mounted Cavalier, *c. 1951*

look at Denham Maclaren's glass and zebra-skin armchair without a smile, though close by is Robert Gibbings's stone sculpture of a Tahitian woman, brilliantly lit, with an overriding sense of strength and power. The museum is particularly keen to highlight works of this century, and one of its temporary exhibition galleries is devoted to shows on diverse themes of modern art and design.

The V & A is divided into various thematic galleries. The Art and Design galleries present all manner of objects to show the art and design made in a particular place or at a particular time: 'The Art of Islam', for example, contains a superb collection of Turkish carpets, Syrian glass, perfume-burners, and tiles to illustrate the culture based on the religion of Islam. The Materials and Techniques Galleries concentrate on particular types of objects, for example ceramics, or ironwork. The Special Collections bring together objects of outstanding importance, from the national collection of musical instruments to a particularly well-chosen display of fakes and forgeries, which has an entertaining collection of imitation and bogus pieces, many created by deceitful and greedy makers or dealers. The mosaic floor of the latter gallery was laid by women inmates of Woking Prison. In addition, a number of rooms in both the main building and Henry Cole

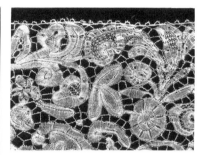
Detail of Irish needlelace, 1886

Wing are devoted to a wide variety of temporary exhibitions.

People go to the V & A for all sorts of reasons. Scholars attend to look at the great study collections, or to consult the National Art Library (one of the world's best collections of artists' illustrated books, and books on art). Many people are drawn by the regular gallery talks and special events. Some come just to be seen at the particularly fashionable temporary exhibitions, others to show off their designer outfits in the costume gallery. Although certain exhibitions do draw very large numbers, it is still possible to find quiet corners throughout the museum, where the display of objects as works of art in their own right makes for an intimate approach, despite the scale of the building and the sheer numerical weight of the collections.

The Wallace Collection

*Hertford House, Manchester Square,
London W1M 6BN   01-935 0687*
⊖ Marble Arch, Bond Street,
Baker Street, Oxford Circus
Open daily. ▣
♿ X G: ramp for front entrance,
lift to first floor; wheelchair
available.
▥ & ♟ contact Museum Assistant
in advance; maximum 25 people.

The Wallace Collection, like other distinguished London private collections in historic houses, retains the feel of a grand home as much as that of a traditional museum. It was bequeathed to the British nation by Lady Wallace in 1897, and is a notable example of a major 19th century fine and decorative art collection.

It was created by Sir Richard Wallace and the third and fourth Marquesses of Hertford, both in London and Paris. The third Marquess advised the Prince Regent on collecting works of art, bought judiciously himself, and had the misfortune of being characterised in fiction, both by Thackeray and

Disraeli, as a sinister and dissolute figure. The fourth Marquess was even more devoted to adding to an already important collection of Dutch paintings, French furniture, French and Italian bronzes, and Sèvres porcelain, with such enthusiam that it acquired a European reputation for its quality and size. The Marquess bought important 17th century European oil paintings, tapestries and sculpture, and his son Richard Wallace continued the fervour of collecting in a manner made possible by his great wealth. It was Richard Wallace who made the departure of collecting works of arms and armours, and added illuminated manuscripts and Italian maiolica pottery. By 1880 the Wallace Collection was virtually completed, and Sir Richard Wallace is known to have contemplated giving it to the British nation. It was Lady Wallace who eventually bequeathed it to the nation, stressing the condition that the collection 'shall be kept together, unmixed with other objects of art'. Her wish has determined that the Wallace Collection remains entirely static and on display; no works can be borrowed from it, and no works added.

The Wallace Collection is housed in

Antoine Coysevox, Charles LeBrun, *1676*

a building known originally as Manchester House, erected between 1776 and 1788 for the fourth Duke of Manchester. In its time it was leased as the Spanish Embassy (1791–95) and the French Embassy (1834–51). Sir Richard Wallace eventually settled in the Manchester Square property in 1875, renamed it Hertford House, and extended part of the building so that the additional art collection made in France could be displayed. Today the museum consists of twenty-five galleries, displaying what is one of the most extraordinary and rich private collections on public display in the world. The collections are described in detail, room by room, in a handy well-illustrated *General Guide*, on sale in the museum bookshop.

The overriding impression of a visit to the Wallace Collection is one of opulence, richness, and the colour of gold. Almost everything on display, it seems, is touched by gold and precious metals, whether on the elaborately-carved frames of French paintings, the gilt-bronze mounts on French 18th century furniture, or even on the chased, iron and gilt-bronze balustrade flanking the Grand Staircase. Originally made for the King's Library in the Palais Mazarin in Paris, the balustrade was sold as scrap-iron during reconstruction work; ironically, it is regarded today as the finest achievement of French iron and bronze work of the 1730s.

Even the guns and armour have

Roll-top desk by J.-H. Riesener, 1769

been collected as works of art, and are displayed to show their marvellous and intricate detail. There is an enchanting scene, for example, of courtly musicians in a pastoral setting inlaid in stag horn on the butt of a wheel lock rifle made around 1600 (catalogue no. A1087). Lecterns standing in the galleries allow visitors to consult in detail the catalogue of the Collection, where meticulously-researched information about the history of individual works is noted. This is above all a scholarly museum, with an academic feel and lineage.

There are many highlights to the collection. Galleries 5–7 show Sir Richard Wallace's wonderful group of European arms and armous, which concentrates on pieces made both for the parade ground and the battlefield, and on 16th and 17th century swords. Gallery 4 was built originally as a tiled smoking room, and now contains precious examples of European decorative art, such as the gleaming metallic lustre ware pots from Spain, and a prestigious collection of Italian maiolica pottery (also shown in the back corridor). There is a rich and substantial display of 18th century painting and furniture in Gallery 21, including a sumptuous kingwood chest of drawers made in 1739 for Louis XV's bedroom at Ver-

The Avignon clock

sailles, and a very important collection of paintings by the French artist, Fragonard. Fragonard's 'The Swing' is perhaps the best known, even if the subject (probably the work's patron ogling his lady) seems in rather poor taste today.

No memory of a visit to the Wallace Collection would be complete without the chime of one of the large numbers of fine, ornate clocks. Outstanding examples are the Avignon clock (F258) in Gallery 22, made as a gift from the city of Avignon to the Marquis of Rochechouart in 1771, and the extraordinary Régulateur clock in Gallery 14, with its complex astronomical movements.

Gallery 19 is a vivid reminder of the large and notable collection of European paintings on display throughout the museum. There are stunning works by great artists (Rembrandt, Titian, Poussin and Claude included), as well as the painting by which the Wallace Collection is known world-wide, 'The Laughing Cavalier' painted by Frans Hals in Haarlem in 1624 (though the picture didn't acquire its current title until the 1870s). This gallery was purpose built by Wallace, and is the largest room at Hertford House. It is a good starting point for a complete tour of the house, since the grand sweep of the room gives a clear impression of the size, scope and visual richness of this extraordinary collection.

Frans Hals, The Laughing Cavalier, *1624*

Wandsworth Museum

Disraeli Road, Putney, London
SW15 2DR   01-871 7074
⊖ East Putney ⇌ Putney
Closed every morning and all day
Thursday and Sunday. **F**
& **X** ground floor, **S** remaining
floors, **G**.
⊮ & ⊮ book in advance; large
groups should arrange to visit in
the mornings when museum is
closed to the public.

From wine-boxes to watercolours,
toasters to tin-glazed earthenware tiles,
the new Wandsworth Museum tells the
story of a London Borough through
everyday objects – and in doing so in a
stylish and entertaining way, makes
that story come to life.

Wandsworth Museum is one of a
new breed of local history museums in
London. It is situated in an attractive, if
slightly fussy Victorian library building
in Putney, and has recently been displayed to high standards of design.
There is a feeling – in the way that the
small museum rooms are full to over-
flowing with objects – for the variety
and richness of everyday life, which
makes a visit here something of a
celebration. Certainly the busy and
well-illustrated narrative panels are excellently written, and provide clear and
thoughtful themes for the visitor to
consider. These new museums take
general ideas of 'history' and make
them relevant to their community: war
and peace, or 'cradle to grave' are seen

Women cyclists in Battersea Park, 1890s

18th century 'Battersea' enamel

in their local context, and illustrated
with some surprising and typical objects. At Wandsworth there are posters
highlighting 'Rat Campaign Week',
beer bottles from the local brewery,
comparative photographs of Edwardian
grocers' shops and modern stores, all
stressing the vitality of ordinary life.

Wandsworth, like many London
Boroughs, has a community that is in
fact a series of smaller communities.
Residents have allegiances to Battersea, Balham, Putney, Tooting,
Earlsfield, Roehampton, Southfields or
Wandsworth, and the museum heeds
these feelings for 'village' life. The
direct involvement of this museum
with its community, and the high regard with which it is held by local
people, are reflected in the way that
residents have donated objects for the
museum collection. There is a strong
emphasis on recording the ephemeral
material – packaging, advertising leaflets, photographs of works outings –
that often does not survive because it is
so common.

Wandsworth Museum has a cheerful
atmosphere and a strong sense of purpose. The mixed nature of the collection makes the visit something of a
visual lottery: there are always unexpected treats to be found, whether it's
the bold and colourful mural, 'Morgan's Wall', on the ground floor, or a
tiny but elegant Battersea enamel. The
museum is clearly laid out. The ground
floor considers the theme of Wandsworth in the 20th century. The first
floor is divided into sections considering life in the area from prehistory to
Victorian times: suburban life; village
and town; and a section on the Thames
and the Wandle, which looks at the
great influence of the two rivers on the
economic life of the riverside communities. Small temporary exhibitions
are held on the upper staircase.

The development of today's
museum as a showcase for local life
contrasts with the history of museum
provision in the area. Earlier this century there were two municipal
museums in the borough of Battersea,

A veiled woman prisoner, Wandsworth Prison, 19th century

Westminster Abbey Museum

Westminter Abbey, London
SW1P 3PA   01-222 5152
⊖ St James's Park, Westminster
Open daily. 🅱 🅰 X G
⚦ 🅵 but must book in advance by writing to English Heritage, Room 429, Thames North, Millbank, London SW1P 4QJ.

Staring into the eyes of King Henry VII is one of the most haunting and elegiac experiences that a visitor to the Westminster Abbey Museum will bring. Meticulous research on the plaster head, now redisplayed in a fine new exhibition, revealed clotting of eyebrow hair from grease used in taking a mould, proving that this head is indeed a death mask. Perhaps that accounts for the eery and heart-rending sadness that the King's quiet gaze creates. (See colour plate 3.)

The success of the Westminster Abbey Museum – and the reasons for strongly recommending a visit – are due to more than being transfixed by one serene and beautiful object. The

museum benefits from elegant and understated design, and its superb historic setting. The current guidebook (which includes descriptions of the Chapter House, Pyx Chamber and Treasury, which can be visited on the same joint admission ticket) shows the Norman Undercroft (dating from about 1070) empty of cases and panels, with its simple yet resonant vaults. The room has had a varied history, including monks' common room, and domestic objects illustrating life in a medieval Benedictine community give a homely touch to the atmosphere of devoted spiritual life.

However, it is the outstanding collection of funeral effigies that makes this such a fascinating museum. It was common from the 13th to the 17th centuries for funeral effigies of dead monarchs and other members of royalty to be carried in stately funeral processions on their way to Westminster Abbey, and then to be exhibited after the burial. It is therefore historically fitting to visit the Westminster Abbey Museum and gaze at such unique medieval wooden effigies, as well as later wax ones. The latter are even more vivid: perhaps most compelling is

and their collections appear to have been much more wide ranging in scope, from plaster casts of the Parthenon frieze to a Maori skirt. A few of these objects have come down to the Wandsworth Museum, and some are displayed, along with items from important collections held by the Wandsworth Historical Society. The latter material is mainly archaeological in nature, from neolithic flints discovered in Putney to Iron Age pottery. Material from the Wandsworth Libraries local history collection complements these three-dimensional objects, and includes prints, photographs, and paintings. The successful integration of all these collections into a bright and entertaining museum that identifies with the needs of local residents has been one of the success stories of London's museum world during the past few years.

The Norman undercroft, Westminster Abbey

The Judgement of Solomon *Norman capital*

are the principal reason for visiting this unusual museum, the patient visitor will discover other carefully displayed objects associated with the Abbey. A commanding sarcophagus (dating from the third century AD) is evidence of Roman settlement at Westminster, and there have been discoveries of fragments of Saxon glass on this site, possibly from an original workshop. One of the most effective and luminous displays in the museum is of later, medieval glass from Henry III's Abbey. The rich depth of colour seems to set a quiet seal of quality on the atmosphere of the exhibition. Anyone who combines a visit to the museum with the spectacular Chapter House and Pyx Chamber, as well as the Abbey itself, will have spent a rewarding, if busy, half-day.

Effigy of Lord Nelson

the richly-dressed figure of Frances Stuart, Duchess of Richmond and Lennox, created by one Mrs Goldsmith, who was known as 'the famous Woman for Waxwork'. An appealing, if rather odd touch to this display, is the Duchess's African grey parrot, which lived with her for forty years and has the distinction of being (almost certainly) the oldest stuffed bird in England!

Mrs Goldsmith is also the artist most probably responsible for the effigies of King William III and Queen Mary II, renowned for their good likeness of character and appearance. These were originally shown in one of the Abbey's chapels by members of the Choir, for a fee. The Choir continued to take a keen (and obviously profitable) interest in extending the collection of effigies at the turn of the 18th and 19th centuries to include popular and famous personalities; effigies of the Prime Minister, William Pitt, and of Lord Nelson are shown at the museum in authentic formal clothes. Patience Wright, who modelled the figure of Pitt, had the dual distinction of being a wax artist with an international reputation, and a notable spy (for the American President Benjamin Franklin). Pitt's dour and tight-lipped expression is no doubt very accurate. There is a more romantic appeal to Catherine Andras's figure of Horatio, Viscount Nelson, purchased in 1806 by the business-like Choirmen, who were anxious not to miss out on the public interest aroused by Nelson's tomb and funeral car at St Paul's Cathedral. Lady Hamilton is known, amongst other contemporaries, to have declared the effigy a very careful and realistic likeness, despite the fact that Nelson has been given the wrong blind eye (it should be the right eye).

Although the elegant cases of effigies, harmoniously arranged and skilfully lit in the arches of the undercroft,

William Morris Gallery and Brangwyn Gift

Lloyd Park, Forest Road, London E17 4PP   01-527 5544 ext.4390
⊖ Walthamstow Central
Closed Mondays, and Sundays other than the first Sunday of each month. 🇫 🇵
& **A G**: ground floor accessible, steps to first floor; phone for further information.
♿ & 🚻 phone Assistant Keeper in advance.

It is difficult not to think about William Morris without imagining a great whirlpool of creative and artistic energy. Any list that attempts to catalogue Morris's achievements becomes exhaustingly long, for he worked with equal facility and passion as a designer, author, and socialist.

The William Morris Gallery offers an appropriate and delightful home for this dazzling story of human achievements. Morris was born in Walthamstow, and the Water House (family home from 1848–56) now displays a permanent collection to illustrate the man's work and influence. Morris's creative skills, both as a designer and an author concerned with the decorative arts, had a major influence on the way people viewed their domestic environments at the end of the 19th century – an influence that is still felt today. At the heart of his artistic philosophy was a passionate belief in the necessity of art to everyday life and everyone's lives. He argued fervently on the theme of art for all with a challenge laid down in *The Beauty of Life* (1880) that people should 'have nothing in your houses that you do not know to be useful, or believe to be beautiful'.

The products that could come up to this bold new domestic standard were manufactured in many cases by the influential firm of Morris & Co, in which Morris took a leading role, both as founder-manager and designer. The

A page from the Kelmscott Press Chaucer, *'The Tale of the Clerk of Oxenford'*

work of Morris & Co is amply described and displayed in the Gallery, and takes in all aspects of decorative art design from ceramic tiles to metalwork, stained glass, furniture, and woven textiles.

Morris's pattern of work suited his gregarious character, and the formation of the company is a typical mix of democracy, ambition and wishful thinking. The leading Pre-Raphaelite painter, Dante Gabriel Rossetti, a friend of Morris, described the hesitant beginnings of the firm:

'One evening a lot of us were together, and we got talking about the way in which artists did all kinds of things in olden times, designed every kind of decoration,

Detail of the Lion Rampant *tile panel by William de Morgan*

Walthamstow in 1936, and this collection remains on display in the Brangwyn Room on the first floor of Water House. It mostly comprises Brangwyn's own paintings and etchings, but also includes some attractive domestic ceramics, designed by Brangwyn for Royal Doulton, and paintings by other British and continental artists, including works by members of the Pre-Raphaelite Brotherhood, such as Burne-Jones and Rossetti.

Morris wrote in *The History of Pattern-Designing* (1882), 'I love art, and I love history; but it is living art and living history that I love. If we have no hope for the future, I do not see how we can look back on the past with pleasure'. The achievement of the William Morris Gallery is to turn that reflection on past work into a genuine delight. The museum has not rested on the significant laurels of its fine and decorative art collections, however, and has acquired in recent years a high reputation for the quality and research of its temporary exhibitions – on the designs of Owen Jones, works by Karl Parsons, and the considerable achievements of May Morris, for example. It is one of London's major collections, with the impressive 18th century house surrounded now by formal and bright municipal gardens. A visit to *Vestry House Museum* (ten minutes' walk away) will complement the time spent at the Gallery, telling as it does the local history of the borough.

and someone suggested – as more of a joke than anything else – that we should each put down five pounds and form a company . . . Morris was elected manager, not because we ever dreamed he would turn out a man of business but because he was the only one among us who had both time and money to spare.'

The collection at the gallery pays tribute to this rather diffident group of artists in some spectacularly lovely works, such as the famous Woodpecker Tapestry, designed by Morris himself and woven at Merton Abbey in 1885. In contrast the Kelmscott Chaucer, a great work of printing, shows Morris's dramatic feel for typography, and black and white illustration. The production of this edition of Geoffrey Chaucer's works was undertaken by the Kelmscott Press, founded by Morris in 1891 to print editions of both his own works and those of his favourite authors. The Chaucer has layout and page decorations by Morris, and illustrations by Sir Edward Burne-Jones.

The ground floor galleries in the Water House concentrate on the abundant story of William Morris's life and works, and his political ideology. But the museum also has comprehensive collections of decorative arts by followers of Morris in the Arts and Crafts Movement, which was influential from the end of the 19th century. The collection is strong on arts and crafts furniture (by well-known names such as Ernest Gimson and Sidney Barnsley), and has important designs for stained glass, as well as products by A.H. Mackmurdo's Century Guild (including furniture, wallpaper, and brass).

The William Morris Gallery tells an effective story of the achievements of harmonious cooperation and friendship. The final part of the collections also pay tribute to friendship – this time between the architect A.H. Mackmurdo and the artist Frank Brangwyn. Mackmurdo introduced his friend to William Morris, to show the great man his work, and Brangwyn later spent some time working in Morris's studios. Local interest aroused by the centenary celebrations of Morris's birth in 1934 inspired the idea that led to the presentation of the important Brangwyn Gift to the Borough of

Frederick Hollyer, William Morris and Edward Burne-Jones, c. *1890*

Museums and Collections in Greater London

Information based on *Museums in London*, third edition, Dec. 1987, edited by Simon Olding and published by the London Museums Service, a division of the Area Museums Service for South Eastern England.

Museums shown in **bold** are described fully in the main text of this volume.

Check with museums for details of opening times, admission prices, how to get there, and information on special events and activities. Please note that some of the specialist collections listed below can only be seen *by appointment*.

CENTRAL LONDON

Westminster and the City of London

All Hallows by the Tower Undercroft Museum

Byward Street, London EC3R 5BJ 01-481 2928

The collection (including a Roman pavement and Roman artefacts) illustrates the history of the church and some of the people connected with it.

Apsley House, The Wellington Museum

149 Piccadilly, Hyde Park Corner, London W1V 9FA   01-499 5676

The Iron Duke's London Palace, housing his famous collection of paintings, porcelain, silver, orders, and decoration.
(A branch of the Victoria and Albert Museum.)

Arts Council Collection

South Bank Board, Royal Festival Hall, London SE1 8XX 01-921 0600)

The largest collection of post-war art in the UK. The collection has no permanent exhibiting space; many of the works are on permanent loan to museums and galleries throughout Britain, or included in touring exhibitions.
By appointment only.

Bank of England Museum

Threadneedle Street, London EC2R 8AH   01-601 4387

Collection relating to the history of the Bank of England.

Barbican Art Gallery

Level 8, Barbican Centre, London EC2Y 8DS   01-638 4141 Ext. 306/346

Frequently displays a selection from the Corporation of London's Permanent Collection of works of art (curated at the *Guildhall Art Gallery*). A programme of major temporary exhibitions is also shown here.

British Architectural Library: Drawings Collection

21 Portman Square, London W1H 9HF   01-580 5533

About 400,000 architectural drawings, including some topographical ones, ranging in date from c. 1500 to the present, as well as portraits, busts, models, drawing instruments, medals, furniture, and other items connected with the history and practice of architecture. Temporary exhibitions at the Heinz Gallery.
By appointment only.

British Council Collection

Fine Arts Department, 11 Portland Place, London W1N 4EJ 01-636 6888

A major collection of 20th century British art, including paintings, sculpture, photographs, and works in mixed media, mainly intended for world-wide circulating exhibitions.
By appointment only.

British Dental Association Museum

64 Wimpole Street, London W1M 8AL   01-935 0875

Major collections relating to the history of Dentistry.
By appointment only.

Cabinet War Rooms

Clive Steps, King Charles Street, London SW1A 2AQ   01-930 6961

The most important surviving part of the underground emergency accommodation used by Winston Churchill and the British Government during the Second World War.
(A branch of the Imperial War Museum.)

Chartered Insurance Institute Museum

The Hall, 20 Aldermanbury, London EC2V 7HY   01-606 3835

The largest collection of UK firemarks and fireplates. Also a collection of artefacts relating to the history of firefighting and fire insurance.

The Clockmaker's Company Collection

The Clock Room, Guildhall Library, Aldermanbury, London EC2P 2EJ 01-606 3030 Ext. 1865

A collection of timepieces, mainly made by members of the Company since its formation in 1631, together with some specialist objects concerned with John Harrison and other great pioneers of chronometry. A major library and archive.

Crafts Council

12 Waterloo Place, London SW1Y 4AU   01-930 4811

Collection of contemporary craft objects, not on permanent display, but available for loan.
By appointment only.

Cricket Memorial Gallery
*Lord's Ground, St John's Wood,
London NW8 8QN   01-289 1611*

Tells the story of cricket from 1550 to
the present day.

Diocesan Treasury in the Crypt of St. Paul's Cathedral
*Chapter House, St. Paul's
Churchyard, London EC4M 8AD
01-248 2705*

Church plate and some Cathedral
treasures.

Dr. Johnson's House
*17 Gough Square, London
EC4A 3DE   01-353 3745*

Where Johnson compiled the first
definitive English dictionary. Exhibits
include portraits, letters, and objects
relating to Johnson and his circle.

The Guards Museum

Guildhall Art Gallery
*Aldermanbury, London EC2P 2EJ
01-260 1632*

The Corporation of London's
Permanent Collection. London
topographical works, Pre-Raphaelite
and 19th century paintings, and
paintings and drawings by Sir Matthew
Smith.
By appointment only, pending rebuilding
(currently scheduled for early 1990s).

Guildhall Library
*Aldermanbury, London EC2P 2EJ
01-260 1839*

The Print Room Collection consists of
prints, drawings, maps, plans, theatre
programmes, playbills, menues, etc.,
relating to London. Also a collection of
Old Master Prints. Small temporary
exhibitions held in the Whittington
Room.
By appointment only.

H.M. Customs and Excise Museum and Exhibition
*Custom House, Lower Thames Street,
London EC3R 6EE   01-382 5574*

Display of artefacts and documents
which reflect the history of smuggling,
cask gauging, and the Customs'
maritime and literary traditions. Also a
permanent exhibition on the
Department's role today.
By appointment only.

The London Toy and Model Museum

London Transport Museum

Metropolitan Police Museum
*c/o Room 1334, New Scotland Yard,
London SW1H OBG*

The collection covers the history of the
Metropolitan Police, London, from its
foundation to the present day. New
museum scheduled to open in
Wapping in 1991.

Michael Faraday's Laboratory and Museum (Royal Institution)
*Royal Institution of Great Britain, 21
Albermarle Street, London W1X 4BS
01-409 2992*

Historic scientific apparatus,
manuscripts, and Faraday personalia.

Museum of the Honourable Artillery Company
*Armoury House, City Road, London
EC1J 2BQ   01-606 4644*

The collection documents the history
of the Company from the 19th century,
and includes uniform, weapons,
equipment, applied art, silver, and
medals.

The Museum of London

Museum of Mankind

The National Gallery

National Portrait Gallery

National Postal Museum

Nelson Collection, Lloyd's
*Lloyd's Lime Street, London
EC3M 7HA   01-623 7100*

Silver and presentation swords
awarded by Patriotic Fund at Lloyd's,
1803–9; silver presented to ships'
captains by merchant underwriters;
silver awarded to Lord Nelson, 1798–
1801 by Lloyd's Copenhagen and Nile
subscriptions. Various letters and
artefacts associated with Nelson.
By appointment only.

Prince Henry's Room
*17 Fleet Street, London EC4Y 1AA
01-353 7323*

A permanent exhibition of Pepysiana
which contains contemporary items,
prints and paintings, depicting the
diarist and the London in which he
lived.

Public Record Office Museum
*Chancery Lane, London WC2A 1LR
01-405 0741 Ext. 229*

The records of the British from the
Domesday Book to the present day,
including records of the royal court,
departments of state and the armed
services.

The Queen's Gallery
*Buckingham Palace, London SW1A
1AA   01-930 4832*

Exhibitions, which change annually,
display different aspects of the huge
and diverse Royal Collection of
paintings and works of art.

Royal Academy of Arts
*Burlington House, Piccadilly, London
SW1V ODS   01-439 7438*

A major collection of works of art,
including diploma works donated by
new Academicians, some on open
display but otherwise *by appointment
only.*

Royal College of Music – Department of Portraits

Prince Consort Road, London SW7 2BS   01-589 3643

Portraits of musicians of all countries. Also houses the College's important collection of concert programmes.

Royal College of Music Museum of Instruments

Royal College of Music, Prince Consort Road, London SW7 2BS 01-589 3643 Ext. 30

Musical instruments, mostly European keyboard, stringed and wind from the 16th and 19th centuries, with some African and Asian instruments.

St. Bride's Crypt Exhibition

St. Bride's Church, Fleet Street, London EC4Y 8AU   01-353 1301

Roman pavement and the various architectural remains from the seven previous churches on this site as well as an historical display on the development of printing and the City of London.

Tate Gallery

Telecom Technology Showcase

Theatre Museum

Tower Bridge

London SE1 2UP   01-407 0922

The Exhibition and Engine Room museum gives an insight into the history, design, function and operation of the bridge.

Twining & Co Ltd

216 The Strand, London W2 01-353 3511

Collection relating to the history of tea.

The Wallace Collection

Westminster Abbey Museum

NORTH WEST LONDON

includes the Boroughs of:
Barnet
Brent
Camden
Ealing
Hammersmith and Fulham
Harrow
Hillingdon
Hounslow
Kensington and Chelsea

Anna Pavlova Memorial Museum

Ivy House, North End Road, London NW11 7HU   01-237 6472

Photographs, programmes, furniture and objects displayed in one room of Anna Pavlova's home.

Barnet Museum

31 Wood Street, Barnet, Herts EN5 4BE   01-449 0321 Ext. 4

Collection drawn from the local community.

Bayhurst Wood Country Park

Breakspear Road North, Harefield, Middlesex   (0895) 630078

The aim of the centre is to demonstrate woodland crafts of the area. The collection consists of old forestry equipment and tools relating to these crafts.

Boston Manor House

Boston Manor Road, Brentford, Middlesex   01-570 7728 Ext. 4176

Jabobean manor house with state rooms upstairs. Used as a venue for local history displays from the London Borough of Hounslow's local history collection and **Gunnersbury Park Museum**.

The British Museum

Carlyle's House

24 Cheyne Row, Chelsea, London SW3 5HL   01-352 7087

18th century town house (Queen Anne) lived in by Thomas and Jane Carlyle from 1834 until their deaths. Furniture, pictures, books and relics belonging to the Carlyles are on view.

Chelsea Physic Garden

66 Royal Hospital Road, London SW3 4HS   01-352 5646

A centre for the study of horticulture, founded by the Society of Apothecaries in 1673 to supply medicinal herbs.

Chiswick House

Burlington Lane, Chiswick, London W4 2RP   01-995 0508

18th century house with ornate reception rooms decorated in their original manner and adorned with some of the original pictures. The ground floor contains an exhibition of 18th century drawings illustrating the evolution of the house and gardens.

Church Farm House Museum

Commonwealth Institute

Courtauld Institute Galleries

The Dickens House Museum

Fenton House

Windmill Hill, London, NW3 6RT 01-435 3471

The Benton Fletcher collection of early keyboard instruments and the Binnings collection of English and continental porcelain.

Freud Museum

Geological Museum

The Grange Museum of Community History

Gunnersbury Park Museum

Hampstead Museum
Burgh House, New End Square,
London NW3 1LT   01-431 0144

Items relating to the history of Hampstead.

Harrow Museum and Heritage Centre

Harrow School Old Speech Room Gallery
c/o 5 High Street, Harrow on the Hill, Middlesex HA1 3HP
01-422 2196 Ext. 225

British Watercolours, antiquities and Harroviana.

Heritage Motor Museum

Hogarth's House
Hogarth Lane, Great West Road,
London W4 2QN   01-994 6757

A permanent exhibition of 145 of Hogarth's engravings plus some reproductions of paintings, in the artist's country home.

Hunterian Museum
35–43 Lincoln's Inn Fields, London WC2A 3PN   01-405 3474 ext. 92

Collection of comparative and morbid anatomy. The Royal College of Surgeons has a definitive collection of pre-Listerian surgical instruments. *By appointment only.*

Inns of Court and City Yeomanry Museum
10 Stone Buildings, Lincoln's Inn Fields, London WC2A 3TG
01-405 8112

Small collection of uniforms, equipment, medals, prints, etc. of the Inns of Court Regiments and the City of London Yeomanry (the Rough Riders) from 1798 to the present.

The Iveagh Bequest, Kenwood

The Jewish Museum

Keats House

Kensington Palace Court Dress Collection and State Apartments

Kew Bridge Steam Museum

Leighton House Museum

Library and Museum of the United Grand Lodge of England
Freemason's Hall, Great Queen Street, London WC2B 5AZ
01-831 9811

Masonic regalia and medals, portraits, artefacts (porcelain, glass, silver) that have been used for Masonic purposes or have Masonic decoration. Principally concerned with English Freemasonry but collections cover Freemasonry worldwide.

Linley Sambourne House
18 Stafford Terrace, London W8 7BH   01-994 1019

A unique survival of a late Victorian town house which still retains original decorations, fixtures and furniture. The home of Punch illustrator Linley Sambourne (1844–1910); an example of a successful artist's house in 'artistic' Kensington.

The London Museum of Jewish Life
The Sternberg Centre, 80 East End Road, Finchley, London N3 2SY
01-346 2288 01-349-1143

The Museum is concerned to recover and preserve material relating to Jewish social history, including working life, domestic life, religion and politics, in England and in the countries from which the Jewish community in England originated.

Museum of Zoology and Comparative Anatomy
University College, Gower Street, London WC1E 6RT   01-387 7050

A teaching and research collection of zoological materials of historic and scientific interest. Also palaeontological collection. *By appointment only.*

The Musical Museum
368 High Street, Brentford, Middlesex TW8 OBD
01-560 8108

Collection of re-enacting and reproducing pianos and other related instruments, tracing their development from the beginning of this century.

National Army Museum

Natural History Museum

Osterley Park House
Osterley, Middlesex TW7 2RL
01-560 3919

One of the finest Robert Adam houses in the country.
(Branch of the Victoria and Albert Museum.)

Percival David Foundation of Chinese Art

The Petrie Museum of Egyptian Archaeology
University College London, Gower Street, London WC1E 6BT
01-387 7050 Ext. 2884

Large collection of Ancient Egyptian antiquities derived chiefly from the excavations of W.M. Flinders Petrie, his colleagues and successors from 1884 to the present day.

Pitshanger Manor Museum

The Polish Institute and Sikorski Museum
20 Princes Gate, London SW7 1PT
01-589 9249

Polish militaria, Polish art, historical archives and a library.

Pollock's Toy Museum

Royal Air Force Museum

Royal College of Physicians
11 St Andrew's Place, Regent's Park, London NW1 4LE
01-935 1174 ext. 374

Around 350 paintings, busts, medals, and miniatures from the 16th to the 20th centuries, mostly portraits of medical and scientific personalities. *By appointment only*.

Royal Hospital Chelsea
Royal Hospital Road, Chelsea, London SW3 4SL
01-730 0161 Ext. 203

Founded in 1682 as a retreat for veterans of the regular army. Small collection of objects relating to the history of the Hospital, and a medal collection.

The Saatchi Collection
98a Boundary Road, London NW8 ORH　01-624 8299

Founded in 1970. Comprises various works by contemporary artists such as Warhol, Malcolm Morley, Richard Serra, which are shown on a rotating basis.

Science Museum

Sir John Soane's Museum

Syon House
Syon Park, Brentford, Middlesex TW8 8JG　01-560 0881

Fine suite of rooms by Robert Adam and an important collection of paintings including works by Gainsborough and Reynolds, Van Dyck and Lely.

Thomas Coram Foundation for Children
40 Brunswick Square, London WC1N 1AZ　01-278 2424

Built on the site of the original Foundling Hospital; contains an important collection of 18th century paintings.

University College Art Collections
Strang Print Room, University College, Gower Street, London WC1E 6BT　01-387 7050

An important collection of fine art, built up from gifts and bequests, including European prints, drawings and paintings, Japanese prints and sculptures by Flaxman. Works are displayed in the Flaxman Gallery and the Strang Print Room (which is also a study area).

Victoria and Albert Museum

NORTH EAST LONDON

includes the Boroughs of:
Barking and Dagenham
Enfield
Hackney
Haringey
Havering
Islington
Newham
Redbridge
Tower Hamlets
Waltham Forest

Bethnal Green Museum of Childhood

Bruce Castle Museum

Epping Forest Museum and Queen Elizabeth's Hunting Lodge
Rangers Road, Chingford, London E4 7QH　01-529 6681

The Museum is housed in a Tudor royal hunting-grandstand and the displays illustrate the history and wildlife of Epping Forest.

Forty Hall
Forty Hill, Enfield, Middlesex 01-363 8196

Local history and fine and applied art.

Geffrye Museum

Hackney Museum

The Heralds' Museum at the Tower of London
H.M. Tower of London, London EC3N 4AB
01-584 0930　01-236 9857

The Museum aims to explain heraldry and to exhibit some of the best examples of applied heraldry, such as heraldic manuscripts and heraldry used on glass, precious metals, porcelain and textiles.

The Heritage Centre, Spitalfields
19 Princelet Street, London E1 6HQ 01-377 6901

A resource centre and museum for the study of immigration with particular reference to the Huguenot, Jewish and Bengali communities who have settled in the Spitalfields area.

John Wesley's House

The London Gas Museum
North Thames Gas, Twelvetrees Crescent, Bromley-by-Bow, London E3　01-987 2000 Ext. 3344

Collection relating to the history of the gas industry.

Middlesex Regimental Museum

Bruce Castle, Lordship Lane, London N17 8NU   01-808 8772

A collection showing all periods of the Regiment's history (see **Bruce Castle Museum**).

Museum in Docklands

Visitor Centre, W Warehouse, Royal Victoria Dock, London E16 01-515 1162

The museum will tell the story of London as a major port and commercial centre, with displays of material relating to cargo handling and dock, boat and river trades.
By appointment only, but there are special events and open days – 'phone for details.

Museum of Methodism, see John Wesley's House

Museum Nature Reserve and Interpretative Centre

Norman Road, East Ham, London E6 4HN   01-470 4525

Nine acre churchyard containing many species of birds, animals and plants.

Museum of the Order of St. John

North Woolwich Old Station Museum

Passmore Edwards Museum

Romford Road, Stratford, London E15 4LZ   01-519 4296

The museum is concerned with the heritage of the geographical county of Essex, especially that area which is now administered by the five London Boroughs north of the River Thames and east of the River Lea, as well as the western part of the administrative county of Essex. Its particular fields of interest are archaeology and local history, biology and geology.

Ragged School Museum

46–48 Copperfield Road, Bow, London E3 4RR   01-232 2941

Late Victorian canalside warehouses converted for use as Ragged School by Dr. Barnardo, then occupied by Jewish clothing industry. Collection will cover objects relating to local history, industry and life in the East End.
By appointment only.

Royal Armouries

Royal Fusiliers Museum

H.M. Tower of London, London EC3N 4AB   01-480 6082

Artefacts and narrative illustrating the history of the Royal Fusiliers from their foundation in 1685 to the present day.

Silver Studio Collection

Middlesex Polytechnic, Bounds Green Road, London N11 2NQ 01-368 1299 Ext. 7339/7397

A comprehensive collection of decorative design material, with designs, wallpapers, design samples and wallpaper pattern books, documenting the work of the Silver Studio of Design.
By appointment only.

Tower of London

Tower Hill, London, EC3N 4AB 01-709 0765

The Tower, begun in the 11th century, has been fortress, palace and prison. Today it houses the **Royal Armouries** and the Crown Jewels.

Upminster Tithe Barn

Hall Lane, Upminster, Essex (0708) 46040

Collections of agricultural material

Upminster Windmill

St. Mary's Lane, Upminster, Essex (0708) 46040

Restored early 19th century smockmill.

Valence House Museum

Becontree Avenue, Dagenham, Essex RM8 3HT   01-592 2211

Items of local history interest plus the Fanshawe family portraits.

Vestry House Museum

Vestry Road, Walthamstow, London E17 9NH 01-509 1917 01-527 5544 Ext. 4391

Collections relating to the history of the London Borough of Waltham Forest.

William Morris Gallery and Brangwyn Gift

SOUTH WEST LONDON

includes the Boroughs of:
Kingston upon Thames
Lambeth
Merton
Richmond upon Thames
Sutton
Wandsworth

The Black Cultural Archives/ Museum

378 Coldharbour Lane, Brixton, London SW9 8LR   01-733 3044

A permanent collection, including African artefacts, slave papers, records and photographs telling the story of Black people in Britain.
Scheduled to open in 1989.

The Embroiderers' Guild

Apartment 41, Hampton Court Palace, East Molesey, Surrey KT8 9AU   01-943 1229

British and foreign embroidery from the 16th century to the present day.
By appointment only.

Florence Nightingale Museum
Gassiot House, 2 Lambeth Palace Road, London SE1 7EW
01-620 0374

Collection of personal memorabilia and other items relating to the life and times of Florence Nightingale. With facilities for research. Scheduled to open in 1989.

Ham House
Ham Street, Richmond, Surrey TW10 7RS   01-940 1950

17th century home of the Duke and Duchess of Lauderdale, with a well documented collection of furniture. (Branch of the Victoria and Albert Museum.)

Hampton Court Palace
East Molesey, Surrey KT8 9AU
01-977 8441

Tudor Palace of Henry VIII with later additions by Sir Christopher Wren. State Apartments, Mantegna cartoons, Maze and Great Vine of historic importance.

Kew Palace
Kew Gardens, Richmond, Surrey

Built in 1631, the Palace today reflects the private lives of George III and Queen Charlotte, who used it as their family retreat.

Kingston Upon Thames Museum and Heritage Centre

The London Taxi Museum
1–3 Brixton Road, London SW9 6DJ
01-735 7777

A small collection of vintage taxis and their prototypes from 1907 to the present.

Marble Hill House
Richmond Road, Twickenham, Middlesex TW1 2NL
01-892 5115

Palladian villa by the Thames, built 1724–9 for Henrietta Howard, mistress of George II, now furnished with paintings and furniture of the period, including works by Hayman, Gravelot, Reynolds, Wilson and Panini.

Marianne North Gallery
Royal Botanic Gardens, Kew, Richmond, Surrey TW9 3AB
01-940 1171

Collection of flower paintings by Marianne North.

Museum of the Moving Image

Museum of Garden History
St. Mary-at-Lambeth, Next Lambeth Palace, Lambeth Palace Road, London SE1 7JU   01-261 1891

History of the Tradescants, father and son, and general garden history.

Museum of the Pharmaceutical Society of Great Britain
1 Lambeth High Street, London SE1 7JN   01-735 9141

Collection relating to the history of pharmacy housed in the headquarters of the Pharmaceutical Society of Great Britain.
By appointment only.

Museum of Richmond
Old Town Hall, Whittaker Avenue, Richmond, Surrey TW9 1TT
01-332 1141

Displays cover the history of the area of Richmond, Kew, Petersham and Ham, and the life of its people.

Orleans House Gallery

The Puppet Centre Trust
Battersea Arts Centre, Lavender Hill, London SW11 5TJ   01-228 5335

A nationally important collection of puppets from all countries and cultures including a commissioned collection of the work of contemporary British puppet makers.
By appointment only.

Royal Military School of Music
Kneller Hall, Kneller Road, Twickenham, Middlesex TW2 7DU
01-898 5533

Wind and stringed instruments of the 17th century onwards as used in military bands.
By appointment only.

Soseki Museum in London
80b The Chase, London SW4
01-720 8718

Museum devoted to the distinguished Japanese novelist Soseki Natume.

The Vintage Wireless Museum
23 Rosendale Road, West Dulwich, London SE21 8DS   01-670 3667

Collection of about 1000 radios and televisions, most pre-war (1917–1940).
By appointment only.

Wandsworth Museum

Whitehall, Cheam
1 Malden Road, Cheam, Sutton, Surrey SM3 8QD   01-643 1236

An historic house with small permanent displays of material from local excavations.

The Wimbledon Lawn Tennis Museum
The All England Club, Church Road, London SW19 5AE   01-946 6131

Memorabilia relating to the history and development of the game of Lawn Tennis from mid-Victorian England to the 1980s.

The Wimbledon Society Museum
26 Lingfield Road, Wimbledon, London SW19   01-540 1153

Wide range of material of local interest including archaeology, watercolours and natural history, relating to the Wimbledon area.
By appointment only.

Wimbledon Windmill Museum

*Windmill Road, Wimbledon
Common, London SW19 5NR
01-947 2825*

The history of windmills and
windmilling told in pictures, models
and the machinery and tools of the
trade.

Wood Museum

*Royal Botanic Gardens, Kew,
Richmond, Surrey TW9 3AB
01-940 1171*

Collection of various types of wood.

SOUTH EAST LONDON

includes the Boroughs of:
Bexley
Bromley
Croydon
Greenwich
Lewisham
Southwark

Bankside Gallery

*48 Hopton Street, London SE1 9JH
01-928 7521*

Collections of the Royal Society of
Painters in Watercolours and Royal
Society of Painter-Etchers and
Engravers.

Bethlem Royal Hospital Archives and Museum

*The Bethlem Royal Hospital, Monk's
Orchard Road, Beckenham, Kent
BR3 3BX   01-777 6611*

Archives of the Bethlem Royal
Hospital and the Maudsley Hospital.
Collection of pictures related to
psychiatry.
By appointment only.

Bexley Museum

*Hall Place, Bourne Road, Bexley,
Kent DA5 1PQ   (0322) 526574
Ext. 221*

The background to the London
Borough of Bexley, with exhibitions on
local history subjects.

Boxing Museum

*Thomas-a-Becket Public House, 320
Old Kent Road, London SE1 5UE
01-703 2644*

Various artefacts relating to boxing past
and present.

Bromley Museum

*The Priory, Church Hill, Orpington
BR6 OHH (0689) 31551*

Collections include part of those
amassed by Sir John Lubbock, first
Lord Avebury, comprising prehistoric
material from Britain and Europe with
comparative ethnographic material
particularly from Australia and the
Pacific Islands. Archaeological
collections from the borough, a small
but locally important geological
collection, and expanding collections
of social history, dress and fine art.

Brunel's Engine House

*St Marychurch Street, Rotherhithe,
London SE16 4JH 01-387 2489/
(0322) 25725*

The Engine House was part of the
temporary works for Brunel's Thames
Tunnel, the world's first underwater
thoroughfare. The tunnel remains in
use by London Underground and the
Engine House is now a museum
housing a restored steam engine and a
display about the Thames Tunnel.
By appointment only.

The Charles Darwin Memorial Museum

Croydon Natural History and Scientific Society

*c/o 96a Brighton Road, South
Croydon, Surrey CR2 6AD
01-688 2720*

Collections relating to local geology,
archaeology, natural and social history.

Crystal Palace Museum

*Anerley Hill, Crystal Palace, London
SE19   01-676 0700*

Located within the last surviving
building of London's Crystal Palace,
the museum will have permanent and
changing displays, focusing on the 85-
year story of the Palace (1851–1936),
highlighting its social impact.

Cuming Museum

*155–157 Walworth Road, London
SE17 1RS   01-703 3324 Ext. 32*

General collection made by R. and
H.S. Cuming between 1782 and 1902,
and subsequent acquisitions relating to
the history and archaeology of
Southwark. There is also a special
display of London superstitions.

The Cutty Sark

Design Museum

*Studio 4.04, 45 Curlew Street,
London SE1 2ND 01-403 6933*

Mass-produced consumer goods from
around the world. The policy of the
museum will be to illustrate the
significant styles and key developments
of 20th century mass-produced design.
Scheduled to open in 1989.

Dulwich Picture Gallery

Erith Museum

*Erith Library, Walnut Tree Road,
Erith DA8 1RS (0322) 336582*

The local history of the Thames-side
town of Erith, from prehistory to
modern history.

The Fan Museum

*c/o 6 Turnpin Lane, Greenwich,
London SE10 9JA   01-305 1441*

A major collection of fans and fan
leaves, the earliest dated 1636, from
many countries (mainly Europe), with
related and explanatory material.
Scheduled to open in 1989.

Greenwich Borough Museum

Plumstead Library, 232 Plumstead High Street, London SE18 1JL 01-855 3240

Archaeology, social history and natural history of the London Borough of Greenwich, which includes, besides Greenwich itself, the local centres of Woolwich, Eltham, Deptford, Charlton, Plumstead and the new town of Thamesmead.

Government Art Collection

St Christopher House Annexe, Sumner Street, London SE1 9LA 01-928 9403

One of the largest holdings of British Art of all periods; works are on display in British government buildings at home and abroad.
By appointment only.

H.M.S. Belfast

Morgan's Lane, Off Tooley Street, London Bridge, London SE1 2JH 01-407 6434

World War II cruiser preserved as a floating naval museum: seven decks showing how sailors lived and worked. (Branch of Imperial War Museum.)

The Horniman Museum and Library

Imperial War Museum

India Office Library and Records

197 Blackfriars Road, London SE1 8NG   01-928 9531

One of the oldest research institutions, originating in the records of the East India Company. Major collections (for example of paintings, drawings and manuscripts) relating to the Indian sub-continent and South East Asia. (Branch of the British Library.)

Livesey Museum

Metropolitan Police Traffic Museum

Catford TDP, 34 Aitken Road, London SE6 01-461 0099

A collection of uniforms, vehicles, photographs and ephemera, which relate to the history of the traffic police. *By appointment only.*

Museum of Artillery in the Rotunda

Repository Road, Woolwich, London SE18   01-854 2242 Ext. 3127

Tells the story of the development of the cannon from medieval days until the present time.

National Maritime Museum

Operating Theatre and Herb Garret Of Old St. Thomas's Hospital

Chapter House, St. Thomas's Street, London SE1 9RY 01-407 7600 Ext. 2739

Sole surviving example in England of an early 19th century operating theatre and exhibits on the history of surgery.

Rangers House

The Riesco Collection of Chinese Ceramics

Fairfield Halls, Park Lane, Croydon, Surrey CR9 1DG   01-686 4433 Ext. 2330

Over 2000 years of Chinese pottery and porcelain represented, from early stoneware to 18th century china for the Imperial Court.

Royal Artillery Regimental Museum

Old Royal Military Academy, Woolwich, London SE18 4DN 01-854 2242 Ext. 3128

The story of the Royal Regiment of Artillery from its formation in 1716 until today.

Shakespeare Globe Museum

Bear Gardens, Bankside, Liberty of the Clink, Southwark, London SE1 9EB 01-928 6342

Models and illustrations depicting the theatres of Shakespeare's London and the new Globe reconstruction scheduled to open in 1992.

South London Art Gallery

Peckham Road, London SE5 8UH 01-703 6120

Paintings, drawings and prints by British artists, and Topographical Collection of 500 paintings and drawings of Southwark.

Woodlands Art Gallery

90 Mycenae Road, Blackheath, London SE3 7SE 01-858 4631

Watercolours and drawings of Greenwich from the mid-18th century.

Index of Subjects

Index of Museum Names

Printed in the United Kingdom for Her Majesty's Stationery Office
Dd. 240075 5/89 C80 3735